Culture DUNDEE

Working in Partnership
with Dundee City Council

REFERENCE AND IN̶ ̶ ̶ ̶ ̶ ̶ ̶ ̶ ̶ ̶ ̶ ̶ ̶ ̶ ̶ ̶Library

ᴀnew this item ̶ ̶ ̶ ̶ ̶ ̶ ̶ ̶ ̶ems
̶renewed
̶othᴇ ̶
ᴊur

Sails & Rigging

Gordon Trower

Helmsman Books

First Published in 1996 by
The Crowood Press Ltd
Ramsbury, Marlborough
Wiltshire SN8 2HR

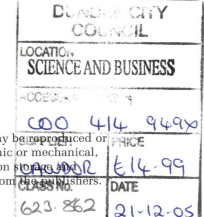

British Library Cataloguing in Publication Data

A catalogue record for this book is available from the British Library.

ISBN 1 85223 853 4

Picture Credits
Photographs by Nola Trower
Line-drawings by Gordon Trower

Acknowledgements
To my wife, Nola, author and photographer, for most of the photographs, for helping with the words, for the dodging in the darkroom and the clattering at the keyboard.

To Rob Tregear for all the question marks in the margin of the draft manuscript, and the helpful suggestions.

To everyone at Penrose Sails of Falmouth for putting up with the photographic disruption.

To Deon Erasmus and Caroline for patiently awaiting design drawings so that the book could be wrapped up first.

To Phil Samuel and *Poldark* for their photogenic qualities.

To Robert Goodden for putting his boat at our disposal.

To Eric White for a balanced view.

To Tim Hope and Giles Frampton for their fine photographs of multiple spreaders and wooden cheek blocks, respectively.

To Riggarna, for the figures used to compose the tables on p.58.

Thank you.

Typeset by MultiMedia Works Ltd, Gloucester
Printed and bound in Great Britain

CONTENTS

INTRODUCTION

At an everyday, superficial level, billowing sails and straining rigging coupled with warm sunshine and a steady force three conjure up an inviting image of relaxed sailing. But underlying this picture of tranquillity, at a more scientific level, those sails are producing a pressure differential providing the propulsive force, the mast and rigging are dealing with compressive and tensile forces in their function of holding up the sails, and the wind is anything but steady.

Serious racing encourages an approach that demands such an analytical perspective. But for all users of sailing boats, the achievement of a level of efficiency in the rig can enhance the pleasure gained from sailing; so this book is aimed also at those who race in a leisurely fashion, those who cruise, those who like to go fast and those who just like to sail. It sets out to explain the concepts involved in cutting and using sails and rigging a boat, in a spirit of enquiry.

From the point of view of the competitive user, the effectiveness of the rig could make the difference between winning and losing. For users who cruise, longevity and strength are of greater concern. With the array of materials available, and the knowledge and skills to use them effectively, both needs can be addressed.

A review of materials and techniques presents the reader with an insight into the changing face of sail-making, particularly in the field of resin films and reinforcement orientation. Aerodynamic theory, research and experience provide some conclusions towards the perfect sail, but neither the sail-maker nor the user can be sure that this is the final word. The time to stop wondering is not yet upon us.

Consideration of the materials available for masting and rigging, and their structural requirements, provides the user with a knowledge of mast sections and rigging layouts. This presents the basis for mast adjustment and adaptation in order to set the sails to greatest advantage. The various systems for rig control call for choices to be made when equipping or re-fitting a boat, and their methods of operation are described.

The need for reliability demands a maintenance programme – as does the high cost of replacing sails, rigging and equipment – and restoration or repair is often feasible. The bonus for the user, apart from the obvious pecuniary one, lies in enhancing problem-solving skills and a knowledge of the way in which materials, systems and components function. This develops a sense of insight that can only add to the enjoyment of sailing, be it in that steady force three or a strong gale.

A number of technical terms are introduced in the text; where they are set in italic type at their first occurrence, a definition will be found in the Glossary.

1
FIRST
CONSIDERATIONS

Naming Names

It is not the intention to provide the reader with the origins or historical context of the terms used to describe parts of sails and *rigging*, but it is necessary to identify the parts by name, as this constitutes 'boat-speak' and ensures some sort of credibility when dealing with the professionals in the field (or on the water).

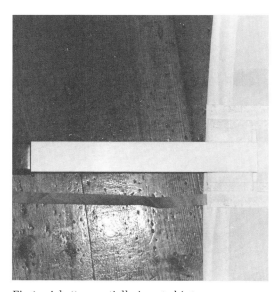

Fig 1 A batten partially inserted into a mainsail batten pocket.

Sail Corners and Edges
(Figs 1 & 2)

Many of the terms are easy to remember. The top of the sail is described as the *head.* The bottom is called the *foot.* The leading edge, or first bit of the sail the wind meets, is known as the *luff.* We also

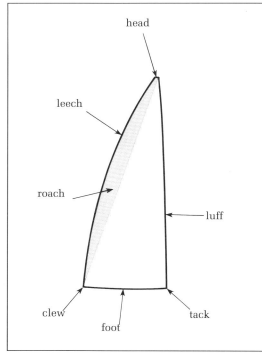

Fig 2 Terminology relating to a triangular sail.

say that when a boat heads towards the wind it luffs, or is *luffing*. The trailing, rear or aft edge of the sail is termed the *leech*. To throw in a curve, the *roach* describes the round of the sail that extends beyond the straight line from the head to the *clew*, which is the lower aft corner. The roach is supported by *battens* that prevent it from flopping over. The remaining corner, the lower forward, is the *tack*.

Sail Configurations
(Figs 3–6)

Sails that are triangular, regarding the leech as one edge of the triangle, are described as *Bermudan*. The classic four-sided sail is a *gaff sail*, the extra edge, known somewhat confusingly as the *head*, being supported by the *gaff*. The very top corner is the *peak* and the corner

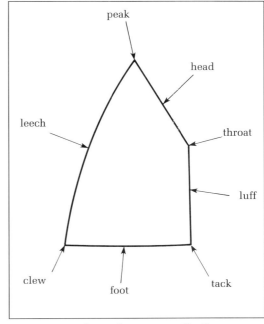

Fig 4   Terminology relating to a gaff sail.

Fig 3   Bermudan rig.

Fig 5   A gaff-rigged boat complete with topsail, which gives a profile similar to a Bermudan sail.

Fig 6   Gunter rig.

between the head and the luff is the *throat.* The remaining terms are unchanged.

A cross between the Bermudan and gaff sail is the *gunter.* The gaff is raised by a single *halyard* (a 'haul-yard') so that the gaff lies parallel and close to the mast. As such, the sail is virtually triangular in form.

Foresails

The three sail types described – Bermudan, gaff and gunter – usually refer to the shape of the *mainsail,* normally the principal sail attached along its luff to the tallest mast. The triangular sail set forward of the mast is termed a foresail. If the foresail overlaps the mast substantially, the sail is commonly described as a *genoa.*

Some yachts possess a choice of foresails, in which case they often are numbered and referred to accordingly: the number 1 represents the largest foresail, the number 2 the next size smaller and so on. Fashion does play a part, and sailors tend to use the terms 'genoa' or 'number 1' (or 2 or 3 and so on). The term 'foresail' is less popular.

Spinnakers and Variants
(*Fig 7*)

A different type of foresail is a *spinnaker,* used when the wind is from astern or from abeam. This sail is fuller than normal foresails and is not attached to a *stay.* A variant, which is a cross between a spinnaker and a genoa, termed a *cruising 'chute,* is popular for cruisers. It is set like a genoa in that the tack is attached directly to the boat, whereas the

Fig 7   Spinnaker set with the wind on the beam.

spinnaker is attached to a *pole* projecting from the mast.

Variants of the cruising 'chute include those more like genoas and those more like spinnakers. High-speed craft frequently have the capability of setting an *asymmetric spinnaker*, which is usually tacked onto a *bowsprit* – a *spar* which overhangs the bow.

Rigs
(Figs 8 & 9)

For convenience in handling, some yachts use two sails forward of the mast, the further forward being termed the *jib* and the aft sail (but still forward of the mast) being termed the *staysail*. To split up the *sail plan* further (the sail plan is the profile of the sails as if pulled into the centre-line of the boat) an additional sail sometimes is set on a mast aft of the mainsail. This sail normally has the same

Fig 8   An unusual rig comprising wing sails.

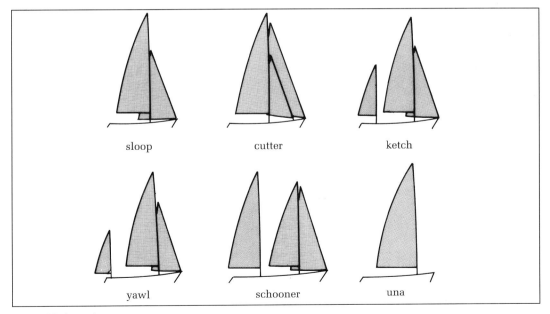

sloop

cutter

ketch

yawl

schooner

una

Fig 9   Various rigs.

profile as the mainsail and is termed a *mizzen.* From the *mizzenmast*, a staysail, known as a *mizzen staysail,* can be set.

The configuration in which a yacht uses a mizzen is called a *ketch* or *yawl,* depending upon the positioning of the mizzenmast relative to the rudder. If the mizzenmast lies forward of the rudder, the mizzen is usually larger and more significant and the boat is described as a ketch. The mizzen of a yawl represents more of an add-on feature.

The most conventional rig is the arrangement using a mainsail and a fore-sail, in which case the boat, whether sailing dinghy, cruiser or super-yacht, is described as a *sloop.* Thus, a boat may be a Bermudan sloop or gaff ketch, which then describes the rig or the layout of the sails and spars (the poles that support the sails). The rig that utilizes a jib and stay-sail already described is termed a *cutter.*

Other types of rig abound. For sailing dinghies, the *una rig* has been popular-ized. This rig uses a mainsail only, for single-handed sailing convenience. At the other end of the spectrum, where a multiplicity of sails can be handled by a multiplicity of crew, rigs such as the *schooner* rig are prominent. Schooners can look very much like ketches, the purist making the differentiation by the relative height of the aft mast – an aft mast taller than, or of the same height as, the forward mast defines the yacht as a schooner. Of course, schooners can and often do have more than two masts and display a variety of ways in which the sails are set within the masts.

Gaff to Bermudan

The way in which the sails can be set depends upon the way the mast is rigged.

For example, the gaff rig was superseded, with intervening steps, by the Bermudan rig through technological development of the rigging. The means of attachment of the mainsail luff of a gaff-rigged boat to the mast was by using hoops. Since the hoops could be hauled up the mast only if there was an absence of rigging up to the height of the gaff, masts were kept short in order that they were not unnecessarily heavy.

The invention of the *mast track* and its accompanying runners attached to the luff of the mainsail – first used on the 6m-class yacht *Gypateos* in 1911 – enabled rigging to be located at any point on the mast. Thus, the height of the mast did not present a restriction, leading to taller, more efficient sails and, of course, the Bermudan rig.

Stays and Shrouds
(Fig 10)

Rigging that supports a mast is termed *standing rigging.* The mast is mainly held up by wires running fore and aft, in which case they are called stays, or athwartships, when they are called *shrouds.*

Thus, the *forestay* prevents the mast falling backwards and the *inner forestay* (or *baby stay)* supports the middle part of the mast, preventing it from bending aft. The *backstay*, otherwise called the standing backstay, provides support from the opposite direction. Again, middle-of-the-mast support is provided by subsidiary backstays, termed *running backstays* and *check stays* because they are freed off on one side at a time to allow the mainsail and boom to be squared off during *downwind* sailing.

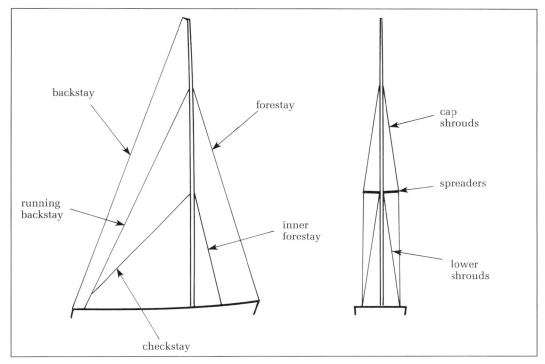

Fig 10   The items of standing rigging often used on a yacht.

Fractional Rigs
(Figs 11 & 12)

Running backstays are favoured particularly on *fractionally rigged* yachts, on which the forestay meets the mast below the masthead and typically at about three-quarter mast height. The running backstays oppose the forestay.

This rig arrangement results in the topmast not being well supported, particularly if the forestay meets the mast relatively low down. A solution sometimes chosen is to use *jumper stays* over *jumper struts*, which prevent the topmast bending. Although defined as stays (and indeed they provide fore-and-aft support) they also prevent the topmast from bending sideways.

Mast Support
(Fig 13)

Some shrouds – such as *lower shrouds*, which provide support to the lower part of the mast – may be displaced forward or aft, in which case they also have a dual function, but we continue to call them 'shrouds' rather than 'shrouds/stays'. Similarly, the *main* or *cap shrouds* may be fixed to the deck aft of the mast and so perform in part as backstays.

Particularly for yachts, *spreaders* are used to spread the shrouds to assist in supporting the mast. The use of two sets of spreaders is common enough, in which case the additional shroud employed is termed an *intermediate shroud*.

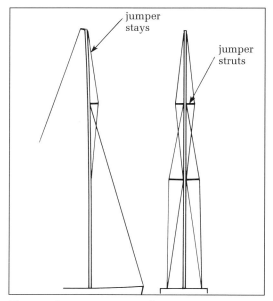

Fig 11   Jumper stays and struts.

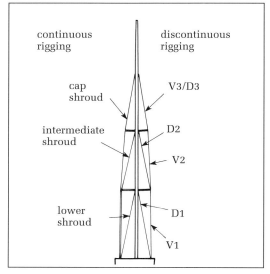

Fig 13   A conventional two-spreader rigging layout (left) and a discontinuous rigging layout (right).

Fig 12   Jumper stays are used to brace the topmast, even though the forestay meets the mast at the same position as the forestay. (The yacht is *masthead-rigged*.)

Discontinuous Rigging

For multiple-spreader layouts, *discontinuous rigging* may be employed, in which the rigging is joined by links at the spreader ends, except for the top spreader. This reduces the number of individual wires. With the use of discontinuous rigging, a numbering system is adopted for the spans of wire that span the points of attachment to the mast. Vertical spans are denoted by the letter V and diagonal spans by the letter D. Numbering starts at the bottom. Thus, the rigging attached to the deck would be denoted by V1 and D1, that from the lowest spreader upwards by V2 and D2, and so on.

Running Rigging

A boat's *running rigging* comprises ropes (constructed either from a fibre such as polyester, or strands of wire) used to set or control the sails. The use of halyards as a means of raising sails has been mentioned already. *Sheets*, a term of frequent confusion for beginners, enable the sails to be pulled towards the centre-line of the boat and indeed freed off. Most other elements of running rigging present refinements only in the setting of the sails.

The Motive Force

It would be rewarding to isolate one principal factor that makes one boat faster than another even though the two are essentially the same. Sailors develop their own theories: the surface finish of the bottom, the *keel foil* or *centreboard*, the weight of the hull or the location of weights in the hull. Most would plump for the sails.

The sails have been described variously as the 'engine', 'power unit' or, more mystically, the 'life force'. Such terms conjure up a picture of the sails as the basic factor affecting speed. Surely the sails must be the element to which racing sailors should give their greatest attention, just as those engaged in motor sport feel that they cannot go fast if the engine delivers insufficient power?

But there is a difference between the concepts of the engine driving the car and the sails propelling the boat. An engine's power can be measured with accuracy using a dynamometer, and an engine tweak that increases the power is realized directly on the car. The capability of the sails to propel the boat cannot be isolated so readily.

Measuring the Power
(Fig 14)

The sailing equivalent of the dynamometer is the wind tunnel. A wind tunnel has the capability of propelling air at a pre-set speed that might range from a light breeze up to strong gale force. One of the principal drawbacks is that the testing of a sail or rig at full size and at reasonable wind speeds would require a huge fan system. We therefore resort to the testing of models of the sail plan.

Scaling Difficulties

Unfortunately, the air flowing over the model rig behaves a little differently from wind past the full-sized rig, and allowance must be made for this. The scaling is not a straightforward process, in the same way that a ship does not rest

Fig 14   A wind tunnel with its dynamometer on the side to measure forces.

on the surface of the water, as does a water-skeeter owing to surface tension. As a result, the wind tunnel provides a less effective means of assessing power than the dynamometer.

Another relative drawback in the testing of sails is that the forces, and hence power, are measured under unchanging conditions: the wind speed is constant, the angle of the sails to the wind is invariable and so on. This represents a poor simulation of what really happens when a boat is sailing in a seaway, given the normal vagaries of the wind. It might be that a sail's shape, developed under test conditions to produce maximum power, proves under real conditions to be inferior because it is less effective overall – less tolerant under conditions that are varying.

Holistic Sailing

A further dimension to consider is the crew, and in particular the helmsman. It may be that certain sail shapes suit some people's sailing style better than others. It is possible that a middle-of-the-fleet crew buys a suit of sails identical to that of the consistently winning boat and that is theoretically better than the original suit, but then the boat fails to maintain its middle-of-the-fleet position.

Over a period of time, given sufficient sensitivity on the part of the crew, they learn how to make the best of the sails, the technique for sailing the boat is adapted and their performance improves, hopefully surpassing their previous efforts. It would seem that the combination and relationship of the

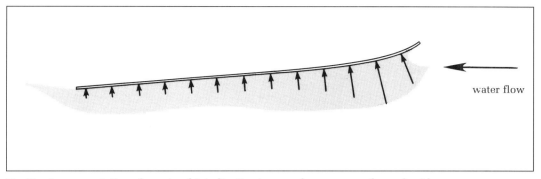

Fig 15   A representation of a water ski, indicating increased pressure on the underside.

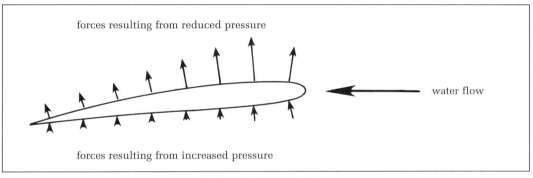

Fig 16   A representation of a submerged foil with flow over both surfaces.

many aspects that affect performance, and the crew's capability to exploit them, are more relevant than the individual parts and indeed more important than uncontested theory.

Wind in the Sails

Of course, much of the theory is well enough substantiated by practice, at least for the general principles relating to sail design if not for the finer points. One example relates to airflow over a sail. Theory suggests that if flow is maintained over both sides of the sail, particularly when sailing as close towards the wind as possible, or *upwind*, efficiency and drive from the sail will be increased.

Pressure and Forces
(Figs 15–17)

A sail produces a force when air impinges upon it in much the same way that a water skier is supported by water striking the skis. This occurrence indicates flow over one side – the underside – only. Pressure in this region is increased and this produces the upward force on the water ski.

However, if we aim to support the person using a submerged foil, shaped rather like an aircraft wing, we find that we can do so at a lower speed or with a smaller area. The water flowing over the upper surface of the foil produces reduced pressure and this has the effect of

15

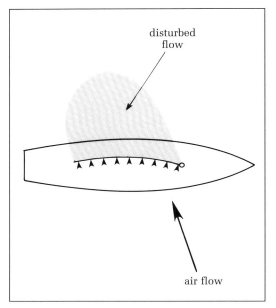

Fig 17   An over-sheeted mainsail with a break-down of flow over the leeward side.

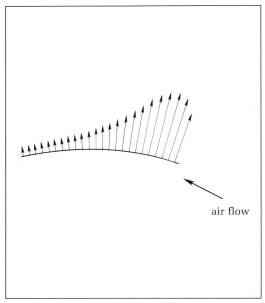

Fig 18   The typical distribution of forces on a sail.

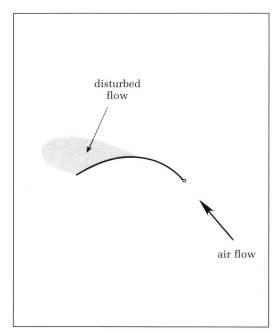

Fig 19   Extreme camber leading to a break-down of flow.

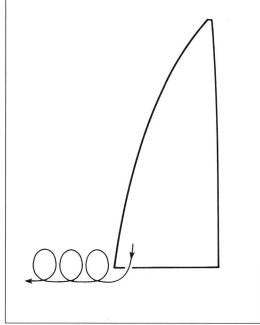

Fig 20   An induced vortex.

sucking the foil upwards, adding to the pushing effect occurring on the underside.

No matter how a sail is *sheeted*, the wind will always push against it on its *windward* side, that is the side facing the wind. But if the sail is over-sheeted by being pulled too close to the boat's centre-line, the air flow is not sustained over the *leeward* or downwind side, eddies are produced and, as a result, pressure is not reduced to the same extent. The wind does not suck as hard.

It is supposed that the air travelling at high speed over the leeward surface of the sail produces a reduction in pressure, which increases the sucking effect. It is convenient to think that the air meets an obstruction – the high-pressure air – on the windward side and therefore tends to be deflected to the leeward side of the sail so that it, the air, is at high speed.

Sail Camber
(Figs 18–20)

Camber, or belly, in the sail encourages this effect. The greatest increase in speed, and therefore the greatest suck, occurs near to the luff of the sail. The distribution of forces on a sail where smooth flow exists on both sides of the sail is shown in Fig 18.

The use of extremes of camber in a sail would seem to be likely to increase the speed of the air over the leeward side and hence magnify the resulting force. However, if taken to extreme, the flow breaks down too readily towards the leech, defeating the object. Another disadvantage is that the boat cannot sail closely enough to the wind, which is necessary if the objective is to make progress upwind. Yet another is that the highly cambered sail produces more side force, which in moderate to fresh winds results in excessive heel. Certainly there is a need to lessen the camber of a sail as the wind speed increases.

Fairly recent research has influenced opinion about the amount of camber used towards the foot of the mainsail. Instead of continuing the camber to the foot to form a shelf, the mainsail is frequently *cut* (at least by those who accept the theory) so that it is flat in this area. Since air travels from high-pressure to low-pressure areas, there is a strong tendency for the air to pass under the boom, inducing a *vortex* or swirl of air. Aerodynamicists have argued that, because this migration is intensified by a large camber, the solution is to reduce camber, since the vortex is a source of drag.

Downwind

When sailing on a reach (with the wind approaching the boat from the side) it is reasonable that the sails are set with greater camber than when sailing upwind. However, when sailing directly before the wind (downwind), camber is less relevant, at least insofar as the mainsail is concerned. Basically, the mainsail serves as a drag system in that the wind pushes on it and there is no continuity of flow on the leeward side.

Although more angled to the wind than the mainsail, only limited flow can be maintained over the spinnaker when sailing downwind. To some extent, a degree of flow can be achieved over the mainsail from the spinnaker, but the benefits are not high.

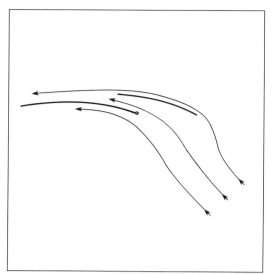

Fig 21   Air flow past the mainsail/foresail combination.

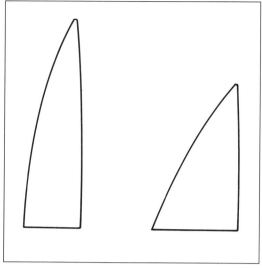

Fig 22   High aspect ratio mainsail (left) in contrast to low aspect ratio mainsail (right).

Sails in Combination
(Fig 21)

When sailing upwind, the combination of foresail and mainsail is more beneficial than both sails taken individually, and the foresail assists flow over the lee of the mainsail. Interestingly, the mainsail enhances the effectiveness of the foresail – which, area for area, produces around 50 per cent more force than the mainsail. The mainsail encourages more air to flow around the leeward side of the foresail.

Whilst it has been supposed in the past that air flows at high velocity through the narrowed gap between mainsail and foresail – known as the slot – theory suggests that some of the air that common sense indicates would pass through the slot is diverted forward around the foresail. Enabling the air to flow smoothly into the luff of the jib is very precious, therefore. Large genoa overlaps are less precious.

High Aspect Ratio
(Fig 22)

The leading parts of sails are very important in that the greatest force is exerted in this region. It follows that a tall, narrow sail will be more efficient for windward sailing than a low, wide sail of equal area. The term *aspect ratio* is used to describe the ratio of a sail's height to average width, the tall, narrow sail possessing a high aspect ratio.

Low Aspect Ratio
(Figs 23 & 24)

High aspect ratio is not always beneficial. Although when sailing upwind a tall sail produces a greater force pushing the boat forward and a lesser heeling force in comparison with a lower sail of the same area, the heeling effect can be greater owing to the leverage of a high aspect ratio sail. Another drawback is that the

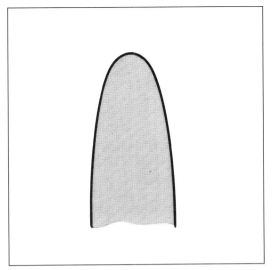

Fig 23   Elliptical planform.

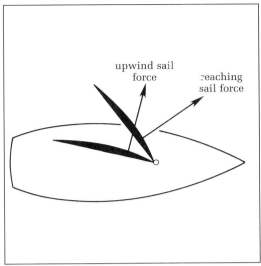

Fig 24   A more productive sail force results from reaching than from sailing upwind.

effect of the interference of the mast on the performance of the high aspect ratio mainsail is relatively greater. Towards the head, the mast can disturb the air flow to such an extent that this part of the sail has little value. The implication is that masts need to have as small a diameter as possible and certainly should be tapered towards the top.

The effectiveness of the high aspect ratio sail can be enhanced by using a large roach. This provides greater width towards the top of the sail, lessening the effect of mast disturbance. Such a sail shape also emulates the classic elliptical 'Spitfire wing' *planform* (its profile), which theory indicates is beneficial.

When reaching, the tables are turned and lower aspect ratio sails produce more force pushing the boat in the required direction. When the sheets are eased, the direction of the large side force existing when sailing upwind is rotated, having the effect of better pushing the boat forwards.

Holding Up the Sails
(Fig 25)

The simplest arrangement for setting the mainsail, particularly for a una-rigged boat, is the use of an unstayed mast. More correctly, it could be supposed that such a rig should be described as non-stayed nor shrouded. Commonly, the bottom or *heel* of the mast is fixed on the boat's backbone and then held at deck level and it is all bend from there upwards. Sailboard masts bend in much the same way, except that the support is at the boom's attachment.

Much more commonly, masts are stayed (and shrouded). The resultant loading on the mast is quite different from that on an unstayed mast. As the wind exerts a force on the sails this loading is transmitted to the mast. In turn this is resisted by the shrouds and stays, which then pull downwards on the mast, placing it in *compression*.

Fig 25   Carbon fibre-reinforced unstayed masts.

Mast Compression
(Figs 26 & 27)

For example, a simple side force on the mast produces tension in the shroud as shown in Fig 26. The reaction is one of the mast having to push upwards at the position of the shroud. It is much the same for the circus big top, or an A-tent for which the poles are under compression.

A compression member of this kind is termed a *strut*. The strut that will stand the greatest compressive load for least weight is a large-diameter round tube. Aluminium alloy mast sections, which are more or less round, meet this

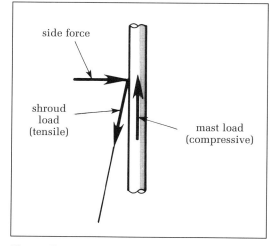

side force

shroud load (tensile)

mast load (compressive)

Fig 26   Representative rig loads produced by the sail's side force.

requirement, whilst solid wooden masts are less successful, structurally speaking. (The *section* is the 'end-on' shape you would see if you sawed transversely through the mast.)

An important factor affecting the load a strut can withstand is its length; if we double the length of the strut it *buckles*

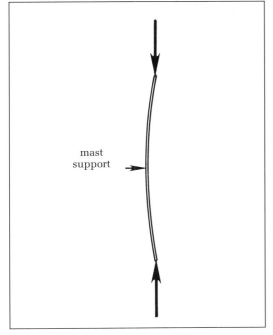

mast support →

Fig 27   Compression in a mast shown split into two panels by a support at mid-height.

with just a quarter of the load. The solution for the mast rests upon providing support at intervals so that the mast is split into a series of struts, termed *panels*.

Extreme bend in the mast will reduce its capability to withstand a compressive load, although if the mast is bent in one particular direction, normally aft at the top and forward in the middle, bracing can be organized more efficiently. The mast can be thought to 'lock out' in this position and as such the condition is stable.

Rigging Tension
(Fig 28)

Although the use of tube for the various items of standing rigging is feasible, the additional and unnecessary windage would be unacceptable. The strength of tensile members is determined by the cross-sectional area of the material and, of course, the breaking strength of the material. Thus, a rod of aluminium alloy having the same cross-sectional area of material as an aluminium alloy tube, and therefore weighing the same, would be equally strong under tension. Of course, bulk can be reduced further by the use of a stronger material, and usually stainless steel is employed.

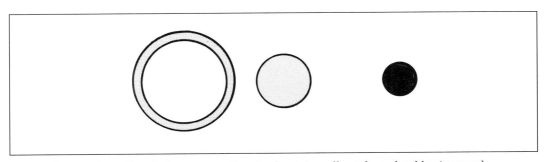

Fig 28   Supposed standing rigging cross-sections in aluminium alloy tube and rod having equal strength (left). For comparison, a rod of the same strength in stainless steel is shown (right).

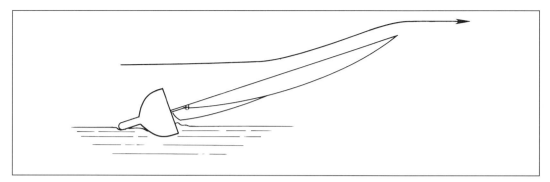

Fig 29   An automatic safety valve.

Stability Effects
(Fig 29)

The strength and therefore size required of both rigging and mast depend upon a number of factors. The boat's stability is an important criterion. A yacht that is *stiff* (does not heel readily) places a greater load on the rig. By contrast, a *tender* yacht heels readily and this reduces the loadings, partly because of the yielding qualities, but also because the wind spills over the sails.

Sailing dinghies tend to break masts when the crew are very heavy or extra crew are carried. Often this occurs when the dinghy is sailing downwind, when the yielding aspect is not apparent. Unlike sailing upwind, the wind cannot be spilled from the sails and the only way of absorbing the loading of a strong gust is by capsizing or by going faster.

The offshore yacht's unavoidable rolling and the crew's good seamanship leading to reducing sail avoid the excesses evident in dinghy sailing. The backstays, both standing and running, also protect the yacht's rig downwind. It is normal therefore to analyse the yacht's rig for sailing upwind. This also is

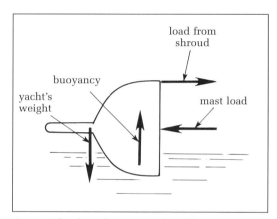

Fig 30   The shrouds on one side of the yacht, in conjunction with the mast, can be seen to heel the yacht.

simpler and we can build in a factor of safety to allow for some of the downwind and other unknowns.

Shroud Loadings and Strength
(Figs 30 & 31)

A very simple approach to estimating the loadings on a mast and rigging is to consider all the shrouds on one side to be pulling the yacht over against the leverage of the mast. Resisting this is the righting effect of the yacht, which reaches a maximum at about 50° of heel. We see

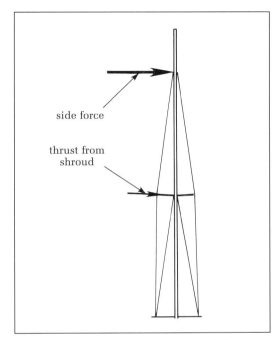

Fig 31   The lower shroud is highly loaded because of the thrust from the spreader.

that the yacht's weight rights the yacht against the leverage of the buoyancy.

In order to gauge the loadings in the rig, we can consider the case of a heavily ballasted, deep-keeled yacht. For simplicity, we can assume its righting effect at 90° is little short of that at a maximum.

The distance between the yacht's *centre of gravity*, where all the weight could be considered to be acting, and the *centre of buoyancy*, defined similarly but for the buoyancy force, is approximately equal to the distance of the shrouds from the mast when heeled 90° (see Fig 30). This implies that the total tension in the shrouds on one side of the yacht is equal to the weight of the yacht.

We therefore need to think in terms of all the rigging on one side having

sufficient strength to lift the yacht. In reality, this would be cutting fine the determination of shroud strength and hence diameter. We need to allow for the unexpected, for deterioration and for the crudity of the analysis presented. We therefore might allow a factor of safety of two to three: we would ensure that the rigging would be sufficiently strong to lift two to three times the weight of the yacht.

This approach is not totally unreasonable for a modern, beamy, lightly ballasted yacht. The maximum righting effect is likely not to be very different from a deep-keeled yacht, but it will occur at a lesser angle of heel and therefore the requirements for the shrouds will not be grossly different.

For a single-spreader rig, the total loading will be split in the approximate proportion of 45 per cent in the cap shroud and 55 per cent in the lower shroud. The lower is more highly stressed because it must oppose the force resulting from the cap shroud pushing the spreader to leeward. If the lower shroud were aft of the mast, its loading would be higher still.

Mast Loadings

Because the mast reacts against the shrouds, which pull downwards, the compression in the mast will be similar in amount to the tension in the shrouds. This implies that the compression in the mast will also be approximately equal to the weight of the boat (visualize the boat inverted and rested on its mast). Again, however, a factor of safety of two to three would be applied for the same reasons outlined previously, to which would be added the contribution the stays make to the compression produced by the shrouds.

The compression in the mast is not uniform down its length. For example, for a single-spreader rig, the length of mast above the spreader to the cap shrouds and stays intersection (the top panel) is compressed by the cap shrouds and stays. However, the bottom panel is compressed not only by the transferred compression of the top panel, but also by that imposed by the lower shrouds.

Dinghy Analysis

Whilst a similar approach to estimating mast and rigging loadings could be applied to a sailing dinghy, its success is less assured. The dinghy is more dynamic and the crew may sail in a style likely to break things. Probably the best solution is to 'suck it and see', particularly as the result of failure probably is less catastrophic and less expensive than for an offshore yacht.

Nevertheless, an appreciation of the kinds of loading involved is of help to those who sail, particularly if they are thinking sailors.

SUMMARY

- The principal terms used to describe a triangular sail are head, tack, clew, luff, leech, foot, roach. Rig types, mostly Bermudan, include sloop, cutter, ketch, yawl, schooner, una. By definition, standing rigging essentially remains unaltered when sailing, unlike running rigging. Shrouds provide transverse support and stays fore and aft support to the mast.

- The sails are but one factor in enabling one boat to sail faster than another. The combination of all factors, including the helmsman, appears significant.

- Sails require camber for efficiency, but, if extreme, flow on the leeward side cannot be maintained, which reduces the driving force. A similar breakdown of flow occurs when the sail is over-sheeted.

- The shrouds on one side need to be strong enough to lift the boat and the mast should be sufficiently strong in compression that the boat could stand on it. A factor of safety of two or three would be applied.

2
MATERIALS USED
BY THE
SAIL-MAKER

Natural Fibres for Sails

If we were able to go back far enough, we would find that the first sails were probably made of bark or animal skins, progressing to hand-woven reeds and palm leaves. Between 3500 and 3000 BC, before the first pyramids were built, linen was being produced in the Middle East, so it is likely that flax sails were being used by the Egyptians on the Nile around this time. Flax is the name given to the fibres of plants of the genus *Linum*, which today can be woven into sail-cloth, canvas, sacking, cambric or lawn, the final product depending on the bleaching, weaving and finishing processes involved.

The flax fibres are particularly long (about 10cm or 4in), making the *yarn* or twisted fibres about twice as strong as cotton yarn for a given weight.

Canvas sails made from flax are heavy, porous and baggy, but reasonably hard wearing because the cloth has no applied finish and so drapes softly rather than forming hard folds. Also, the stitching beds into the fabric, preventing it from wearing out when in contact with items of rigging and other sails.

The use of canvas sails endured for centuries, witnessing the merchantmen of the Mediterranean, the Viking longships, the full-rigged sailing vessels of Magellan, Columbus, Drake and their fellow explorers and, perhaps the most romantic ships of all, the short-lived, graceful tea clippers. Probably the last working ships to use canvas sails were the cargo schooners of the early twentieth century, which plied their trade up and down the Atlantic coast of North America.

Cotton

Viable commercial sailing ships disappeared as steam took over in the nineteenth century, but in 1851 a famous race around the Isle of Wight sounded the death knell for flax sails when the yacht *America* won the Hundred Guineas Cup, henceforth known as the America's Cup in honour of the victor. She was sporting American cotton sails, which were flatter and smoother than the flax sails carried by her rival the British yacht *Britannia*, enabling her to sail closer to the wind and so win by a considerable margin. From then on, the use of flax sails declined and cotton was king for many years.

Anyone sailing before the 1960s will have experienced cotton sails; sailing with them is rather akin to camping in ex-army tents. They stretch and billow in any sort of wind, grow colonies of moulds and rot away to nothing when consigned to a locker for any length of time. Nevertheless, they are very soft to handle and easy to patch together if torn. Nowadays, cotton, and to a certain extent flax, are used mainly for museum pieces and by those classic boat owners who are sticklers for authenticity.

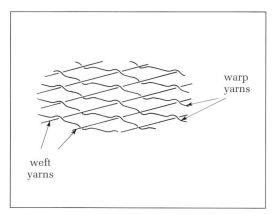

Fig 32   A representation of the construction of sail fabric.

The Use of Synthetics

Nylon
(Figs 32 & 33)

In the mid 1930s, the first nylon of commercial interest was discovered and this changed the face of sail-making for ever. Nylon is a generic term covering the synthetic chemical compounds called polymeric amides, or polyamides, which can be drawn into filaments, these being twisted together into fibres. Following development by DuPont, the first nylon factory began production in 1940 in the United States with a view to the manufacture of clothing.

The weaving of the nylon fibres followed the same principles as for cotton and flax, and indeed the process remains largely unchanged to this day. Long yarns are wound onto a loom to form the *warp*, running along the length of the fabric, through which more yarns are threaded back and forth to form the *weft*, resulting in a fabric with yarns at right angles to each other.

If the warp or weft yarns are spaced out, the resulting cloth is loose and prone to distortion. Conversely, if the warp yarns are laid close together and the weft is beaten down hard as it is woven, the cloth will be tight, stable and less porous.

Stability under load is a most desirable attribute for sail-cloth. When stretched on the *bias* – at an angle of 45° to the thread-line – a woven fabric distorts, and the quest continues for a material with a very low distortion rate, which is what is needed for fore-and-aft sails such as mainsails and foresails.

Another factor that can cause stretch along the yarns (as opposed to distortion on the bias) is the amount of twist in the fibres and *crimp* in the yarns. Crimp is inherent in a closely woven fabric, where the weft yarns are taut and the warp accommodates the weft by distorting around it during the beating-down process. From this it can be seen that woven sail-cloth has more stretch along the warp than across the weft and this determines the way in which the sail-maker orientates the cloth during the sail

Fig 33   Ripstop nylon – showing its age.

designing and making processes. Sail-cloth manufacturers can manipulate the combinations of fibres and yarns, twist and crimp to give a multitude of fabrics suitable for different applications.

The first nylon sail-cloth was rather porous and stretchy, and consequently nylon mainsails and foresails were somewhat disappointing in use and unable to hold the required shape under load. This stretch characteristic was what made nylon ideal for downwind sails, especially spinnakers, which suffer snatch loadings and require a high strength-to-weight ratio. The porosity problem has been addressed by increasing the number of filaments in the yarns, by weaving tightly and by applying resin coatings to the cloth.

A specially reinforced extra-light-weight cloth, generally referred to as 'Ripstop', was developed especially for spinnakers. The cloth has a thicker thread laid at regular intervals into the warp and the weft, giving the appearance of small squares, and acts as a deterrent to ripping. It can be dyed in numerous bright and Day-Glo colours, giving every opportunity to design an eye-catching spinnaker.

Nylon is resistant to moulds, but gradually deteriorates in sunlight – not such a problem for weekend sailors but significant enough for round-the-world sailors who sometimes have to carry downwind sails for weeks on end. Darker colours stand up better to ultra-violet light than white or pale colours.

Nylon is available in a variety of

weights, making it suitable for downwind sails such as cruising 'chutes and multi-purpose genoas as well as light- and heavy-weather spinnakers.

Polyester

Polyester was invented in Lancashire, England, in 1941, but due to the advent of the Second World War the first commercial yarn did not appear until 1944. It was produced by ICI and called Terylene. Companies in the United States bought rights to produce polyester, which the Americans called Dacron. These are the two names with which sailors will be most familiar, as today the majority of cruising sails are made from one or the other. Other countries followed with their own brand names – Tergal (France), Trevira (Germany), Tetoron (Japan), Terital (Italy), Lavsan (Russia) – though you are more likely to find these names on clothing fabrics than sail-cloth.

The chemical formula was identical, but subtle differences in the weaves produced fabrics with different handling qualities. This is important when choosing a cloth for a particular sail. The main attraction of the first polyester sails was that they were virtually impervious to rot and mildew. With further advances in weaving technology, looms were built specifically to produce sail-cloth and an improved cloth of high strength and low porosity in various weights and weaves became the norm.

Cloth Treatment

These improvements are achieved by the way the cloth is treated after it is woven, and the same principles apply to nylon and polyester. The first stage is *scouring*, when the woven cloth is cleaned in a detergent bath to remove the *sizes* applied as lubricants to assist the weaving process. After drying, the cloth is impregnated with resins that 'lock' the weave and so decrease the amount of stretch in the cloth.

The amount and type of resins are carefully controlled according to the characteristics required. Some sails have a hard coating, making a very low-stretch fabric that is suitable for racing as it holds its shape well, but is more difficult to handle and stow because the coating is stiff and prone to crazing. Some American polyester (Dacron) sails have a softer finish, achieved by a tighter weave rather than a resin finish, and these have proved popular for cruising as they are more pleasant to handle.

After the resin process, the cloth is dried again before *heat-setting*, when it is passed through ovens at temperatures up to 210°C. This serves several purposes: it shrinks the yarns by about 25 per cent (which consequently close up to give a much denser cloth), it sets the crimp in the yarns permanently so that the cloth will recover after stretching, and it bonds the resin chemically to the cloth so that it is not just a coating but an inherent part of the structure.

The processes for nylon production differ only where there is a need for dyeing, which calls for it to be heat-set twice, once before dyeing and once after resin impregnation.

The final process is *calendering*, when the cloth is passed between rollers under high pressure, forcing the yarns together so that they mould around each other to form a very stable fabric with a low-bias stretch. Nylon very rarely needs calendering.

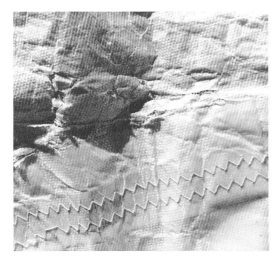

Fig 34   A 1990s' laminated sail showing a breakdown of the resin film after much use.

Fig 35   Mainsail with aramid fibre reinforcement in the leech area.

Fig 36   Laminated sails in action. Note the way that the mainsail is *backwinded* but does not flog. Such sails can be built so that they are as durable as polyester sails, lighter in weight and little more expensive. They are likely to become the first choice for cruisers, in time.

Resin Film-Based Sails
(Figs 34–36)

In the 1970s, something of a revolution occurred. Until then, all sail-cloth had been woven and finishes had been added to make it smooth and non-porous.

The revolution began with experiments using a resin film to make spinnakers for the 1964 America's Cup yachts *American Eagle* and *Constellation*.

Fig 37   A selection of laminates.

This resin film is commonly known as Mylar, its registered name in the United States, but it is also known by its UK name Melinex. It is an extruded polymer that is then stretched to line up the molecules in the direction of what would be the warp and the weft if this were a conventional woven cloth. The result of this stretching is that the molecules become aligned and more closely linked, instead of being random, and this results in less stretch in all directions.

The America's Cup sails were not too successful as the material was far too prone to splitting, but the experimentation continued and in 1977 the 12m yacht *Enterprise* was fitted with foresails made from lightweight polyester with a Mylar film laminated to each side. The thinking behind this was that the woven polyester would stop the Mylar splitting, whilst the Mylar film would stop the polyester stretching on the bias and form a very smooth, non-porous surface. It was successful up to a point, but the drawback was that delamination occurred due to poor adhesion.

Experimentation with cloth, film, resins and glues continued, and by 1980 the choices of laminated polyester and resin film cloths had grown, and consisted mainly of a two-layered construction rather than a 'sandwich', giving less trouble with delamination and a more flexible cloth. Further experimentation produced fabric that incorporated an extremely low-stretch *aramid* fibre named Kevlar – which, due to the difficult manufacturing processes, is very expensive. The greatest drawback of aramid fibre is its inability to withstand flexing, causing the fabric to break.

Combining it with polyester and then applying a resin film produces an extremely low-stretch fabric with a very high strength-to-weight ratio. Because of the expense, this cloth has been banned by some dinghy and yacht class associations for racing, but as durability improves it will become more acceptable, if only for reinforcement patches.

New Fabrics
(Figs 37 & 38)

The present range of laminated cloths is impressive and mainly consists of two- and three-ply laminates in a multitude of combinations. New fabrics have been developed, such as *scrims*, which are lightweight cloths of very open weave, with visible spaces between the yarns. When resin film is laminated onto both sides, it fills the holes and forms a very secure bond. Although polyester fibre is normally used for scrims, other fibres can be incorporated.

Knits are similar to scrims but are non-woven, that is the warp is laid in one direction and more yarns are laid at right angles to the warp, but since these yarns do not weave in and out, they cannot rightly be called the weft. The two are held together by a cross-woven thread, and then again laminated on both sides. Again, various fibres are used. Because of the lower concentration of fibres in scrims and knits, they are relatively cheap to produce, and embody all the characteristics a yachtsman desires: low weight, high strength, low stretch and good durability.

There is another high-performance fibre on the market at present, already accepted for running rigging, called high modulus polyethylene (HMPE), available under the trade name of Spectra. The term *modulus* relates to its effective response to loading. HMPE fibre was

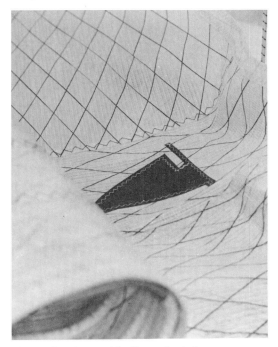

Fig 38 Laminate with diagonal reinforcement in black (though it is not carbon fibre!).

developed in the Netherlands and perfected by Allied Signal Corporation in the United States. It has a greater flex-fatigue life and possesses lower stretch properties and higher strength than the aramids, weight for weight. It also floats. Its one big drawback is its lack of recovery if overloaded. Permanent distortion results if the fabric is loaded to 30 per cent of its breaking strength.

More and more exotic materials are appearing in sails now, such as 'Cuben Fibre' (now re-named F3 – Filament Fortified Film) developed for *America*[3], the 1992 America's Cup's winning syndicate. This consists of a composite of carbon fibre in a liquid crystal film, producing sails weighing up to 40 per cent less than high modulus aramid sails. The carbon filaments have neither twist nor crimp, making for a very thin fabric with extremely low stretch and negligible degradation after repeated folding. With its resistance to ultra-violet light and the huge saving in weight, this is one for the death-or-glory racers.

All the sail-cloths discussed here tend to be used in combination. According to the function of the sail, different fabrics can be used to shape, control and reinforce a sail, and the final choice usually rests with the sail designer, with suitable account being taken of the customer's pocket.

Seamless Sails

So far, the discussion has been about cloth, whether it be woven or otherwise, which then has to be cut, shaped, and sewn or glued together to form a sail of the required shape.

The very latest technology produces a one-piece, seamless sail that has been 'built' in a hangar using an overhead gantry rather than sewn together in a loft. The mechanics of the exercise consist of 'laying up' a polymer film on an adjustable convex mould of the exact shape the designer decrees, and applying filaments of various materials such as carbon fibre and aramids in such a way that they are positioned along the pre-determined tension lines of the sail. After the application of a second film layer, the 'sandwich' is subjected to a heat and vacuum pressure process that results in a laminated sail requiring only edge-finishing and the application of corner reinforcement patches.

This technique is still in its infancy, and therefore prohibitively expensive for the average yachtsman, but the same process could be carried out using polyester threads, bringing the cost closer to an acceptable level for the racing fraternity. Those who cruise are less likely to be impressed.

Summary

- Until the early 1960s, most sails were made from natural fibres, notably flax and cotton. Sails in these materials are heavy, porous, prone to rotting and not very stable.

- The first of the synthetic fibres was nylon. Stretchy in character, this fibre meets the needs of spinnakers and is used nowadays in 'Ripstop' form.

- Polyester, best known as Terylene or Dacron, possesses lower stretch characteristics than nylon, making it very suitable for fore-and-aft sails.

- Resin film-based fabrics have made an impact in the area of high-performance sails. A resin film is reinforced using fibres made from polyester, aramid, high modulus polyethylene, or carbon fibres that can be oriented individually to provide a structured material and a sail with minimal stretch or distortion.

3
MAKING OR BUILDING SAILS

The practice of sail-making changes constantly, with the shift in materials used from cotton to polyester to laminates, the increased use of machining as opposed to hand sewing, the use of lasers for batch-cutting cloth and the use of computers as a tool in design.

Creating Camber in a Sail

Like the design of the hull, improvement in sail performance results more from the technological applications of newly developed materials than from leaps in design thinking. The design of hulls or sails is complex and we do not really know that we have the best solutions, however much the computer may convince us that we have. Building a sail so that the camber is optimal over a range of conditions is one such example; camber is uppermost in the mind of the sail-maker and has more than a passing interest for the programmer.

Sail Response
(Fig 39)

The early use of more stretchy cloths, such as cotton, meant that camber was induced in the sail by the wind. A

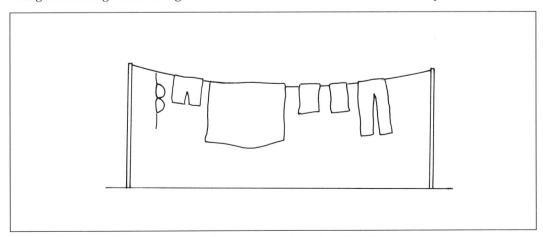

Fig 39   A sail develops camber in a similar manner to a loaded washing line.

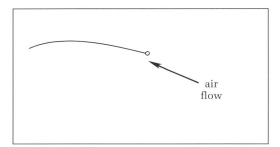

Fig 40   Fullness moves aft at higher wind speeds.

relatively small amount of stretch produced a remarkably large increase in camber. This principle is demonstrated by the hanging of washing on a line. It is impossible to prevent the line from sagging.

Unfortunately, this means of introducing camber is completely opposite to that which we desire. As the wind increases, we want the sail to become flatter, not fuller. The benefit of very low-stretch cloth is apparent. Perhaps the next step will be cloths that have a 'memory' and contract when the load increases. To a limited extent, this effect in which the sail is flattened as the wind increases has been achieved by the cut of the sails.

Luff Round
(Figs 40 & 41)

The amount of camber in a sail is affected by the shape of the luff. By cutting the luff of a mainsail to a convex curve rather than a straight line, excess cloth is available, which creates camber. Where the cloth is fairly flexible, this excess cloth moves aft into the body of the sail. The deepest point of the camber always tends to move aft as the wind increases. For a cloth of low flexibility, this system

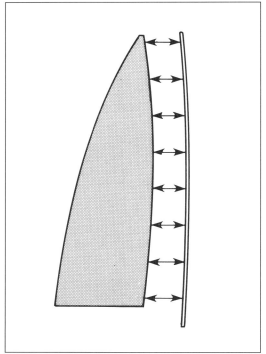

Fig 41   Luff round must relate to mast bend.

of providing camber is less successful.

But a major advantage lies in the way that camber can be varied by bending the mast. As the mast is bent, it moves towards matching the curve in the luff, progressively flattening the mainsail. For example, if a dinghy mainsail is built using 100mm (4in) of luff round, the sail will have zero camber induced by the luff round when the mast is bent 100mm.

For this reason, the sail-maker requires a knowledge of the mast offsets when bent so that an appropriate luff round can be inbuilt. Since the nature and extent of bend can be varied by adjustments to the shrouds, spreaders and backstay, an opportunity is provided for varying the amount of camber induced by this method at different heights.

This curve produces fullness just as luff round in the mainsail does.

In order to limit the camber produced by luff sag, a small amount of hollow may be cut into the luff. This will depend upon the straightness of the luff when sailing. I recall a gaff cutter's jib being cut with some 200mm (8in) of hollow because that suited the curve adopted by the sail when sailing.

Forestay Tension

Because of the way in which this gaff cutter was rigged, great tension could not be applied to the luff. Modern yachts and dinghies, particularly if intended for racing, are set up so that significant tension can be created in the forestay, usually by tensioning the backstays or the aft-swept shrouds.

Nevertheless, the washing line analogy used to describe cloth stretch applies here too. It takes very little washing, or weight of wind, to produce sag in the washing line or the forestay.

This situation is an unfortunate one because it means that, as the wind increases, more sag results and the foresail becomes fuller. This produces increased heeling force – which suggests that, in a gust, a yacht will heel further, not only because of the gust but because the foresail has developed more camber. Worse yet, the fullness tends to shift further aft so that there is more curve in the aft part of the sail and this increases drag, which slows the yacht.

The problem occurs in gusty, moderate winds rather than strong winds. In the case of the latter, the boat essentially is pressed all the time and spills wind in the gusts unless well reefed. In a sense, therefore, the wind feels more constant.

Fig 42   A view along the luff showing sag, which is creating fullness in this genoa.

Foresail Luff Sag
(Fig 42)

The same principle by which camber is created by luff shaping in the mainsail applies also to the foresail. Since the foresail is usually attached to the forestay, or to a wire in its luff in the case of sailing dinghies, round placed in the luff would automatically lead to fullness in the jib.

In reality, round in the luff of the jib is not generally required, except perhaps for a small amount in the lower part. Even when the forestay or the wire luff is highly tensioned, the effect of the wind and the jib sheet causes the luff to sag.

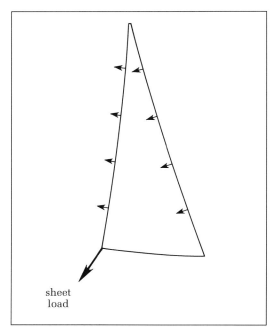

Fig 43   Luff sag induces fullness, which then is reduced by the sheet pulling the body of the sail aft.

Camber Control
(Figs 43 & 44)

A system of correction that is effective, if tiresome, is to sheet in the foresail when the wind gusts and ease the sheet when the wind normalizes or drops. Foresails are cut with less fullness than mainsails because fullness can be induced by easing the sheet, though this would not be successful for a foresail set on a boom, like a mainsail.

Advantage can be taken of the technique whereby sheet tension adjusts fullness. Hollow cut in the leech of the foresail produces a corrective effect on camber. As the jib is sheeted in a gust, the leech is further tensioned. This tends to straighten the leech, pulling the body of the sail backwards and reducing fullness,

particularly in the aft area of the foresail. This is all good news. The only bad news is that hollow in the leech loses sail area.

Fully Battened Mainsails
(Fig 45)

The opposite effect can occur in the case of mainsails, particularly of the *fully battened* type. *Full-length battens* have been used for catamaran mainsails for decades because such craft have tended to adopt large mainsail roaches, and the battens provide support for this part of the sail. Sailboards favour full-length battens too and their use has spread to yachts, in this case because of the ease of handling they confer.

When the leech is tensioned on a fully battened mainsail, there is a tendency for the roach curve to lessen, thus increasing the camber of the sail. However, the wind in the sail reduces this effect – the net

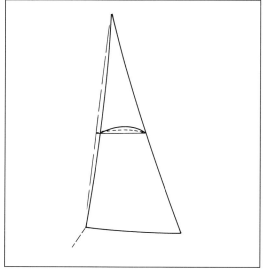

Fig 44   The effect of increasing the foresail sheet tension is to straighten the hollow leech, thus flattening the sail.

The term broad-seaming describes the process fairly well. Seams are used in sails in order to join the panels of cloth, which are woven in a range of widths measured in imperial units – 36, 40 and 54in being typical (914, 1,016 and 1,372mm respectively). Fullness is created by varying the overlap of the seams, making them broader in particular places.

An alternative to increasing the overlap is by re-shaping the edges of the cloth so that, when the seam is formed, the seam edges are parallel. Some would say that this technique is neater and avoids the distortions in the sail that can result from a wide seam. It also ensures that the sail-maker's art remains in the sail loft, not to be revealed except by taking the sail apart.

Tailors use a similar system for creating fullness in clothes. By darting an

Fig 45   Cruiser with a fully battened mainsail.

result, hopefully, being that the sail sets perfectly.

More commonly, boats use *soft sails* in which a smaller roach is supported by relatively short battens.

Broad-Seaming Principles
(Fig 46)

The use of luff round, and other shaping of the edges of a sail, is more suitable as a means of creating camber for elastic cloths than for stable or *structured* materials. For the latter fabrics, camber must be built into the sail by a method known as *broad-seaming*, though a combination of both systems generally is used.

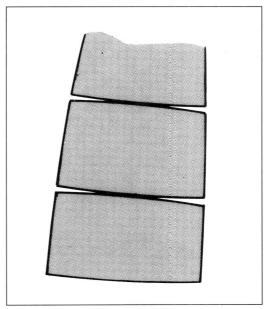

Fig 46   The principle of broad-seaming. When the seams are joined, inbuilt camber is created.

edge of the garment, the edge is tightened, resulting in an excess of fabric in the middle.

Designed Camber
(Fig 47)

Darts are used by sail-makers too in order to create camber, but normally only where too few seams exist in the area where more fullness is required, principally the luff and tack area. Otherwise, the seam simply is adjusted. The end of the dart or broadseam is located where maximum fullness is required.

It would seem logical for a sail to be broad-seamed from all edges, but the leech is not treated in this way. The demand for a fairly flat area towards the

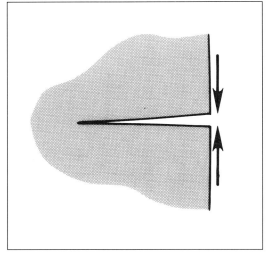

Fig 47 Camber results from pulling the edges of the dart together.

Fig 48 Foot slackened.

Fig 49   Clew outhauled showing the shelf stretched.

leech is paramount because too much camber in this area increases drag. Also, the point of maximum fullness moves aft when sailing – the wind-induced effect already mentioned.

By way of exception, the symmetrical spinnaker (as opposed to the asymmetrical spinnaker or cruising 'chute) is broad-seamed from both of the more or less vertical edges. The symmetrical spinnaker is cut with greater fullness than fore-and-aft sails and must have the capability for flowing air from either edge. Both edges therefore are called luffs.

Camber in the Foot
(Figs 48–50)

Darting or broad-seaming the foot of a spinnaker is common enough, not so

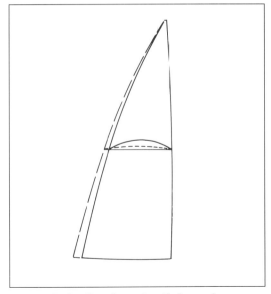

Fig 50   Outhauling the mainsail clew reduces camber.

much to produce fullness but more to ensure that the large round built into the bottom does not flap. The genoa foot is often dealt with in the same way. The same technique can be applied to the foot of a mainsail that is *loose-footed*. With this configuration, the sail is attached at its clew to the boom, but not along the foot.

If you choose not to believe the theory that camber in the vicinity of the boom leads to air migration and vortices, but prefer to believe that the shelf minimizes end losses, then dart or broad-seam away. Better still, though, would be to shape a shelf from sail-cloth, preferably arranged so that it is sufficiently elastic to permit adjustment to the mainsail foot.

As the foot of the mainsail is pulled out along the boom, the distance between leech and luff is increased throughout the height of the sail, producing a flattening effect. Fullness induced by moving the clew inboard tends to be centred between the leech and luff, and this method of creating camber results in the maximum fullness of the sail being too far aft in sailing conditions. However, when coupled with the other two main techniques for producing camber, the result is a sail that can be adapted for different wind strengths.

Luff Tensioning

Another adjustment of significance available to the sailor is the tensioning of the luff. By increasing luff tension, which works both for mainsails and foresails, the point of maximum camber is pulled forward. This is illustrated, perhaps to an extreme, by pulling on the edge of a piece of cloth: folds appear close to the edge.

This provides some control over the positioning of the maximum camber so that it is at least one third but no more than half way back from the luff. The sailmaker takes this effect into account when building the sail.

Appropriate Camber
Fig 51)

The amount of camber required is likely to be in the order of one sixth to one eighth, defined by the ratio of the depth of the camber, termed the *draft*, to the distance from luff to leech at a particular height. A camber of one sixth indicates a reasonably full sail and might be typical of a foresail, whilst a mainsail might be set with a camber of one seventh. More precise values are given in Chapter 7.

Fabric and Reinforcement Orientation

It could be suggested that the perfect sail would be produced on a mould in the same way that fibreglass boats are built, and of a material that stretches minimally

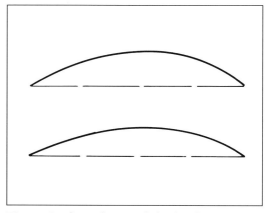

Fig 51   Cambers of one sixth (top) and one seventh (bottom).

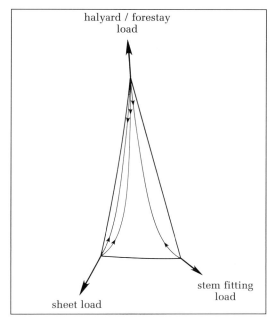

Fig 52   Tension mapping in a genoa.

Tension in the Fabric
(Fig 52)

The problem is not new. Over centuries, sail-makers have sewn sails together, arranging the cloth so that only minimal stretch occurs in the areas of highest tension. Some judgement about those areas of greatest tension in the fabric can be made by prodding a sail whilst sailing. Push it in the middle from the leeward side and the bagginess can be distorted. Clearly, in this region the cloth is under low tension. By comparison, the leech area is pretty unyielding, though the amount of tension in the leech will depend upon how hard the mainsheet or *kicking strap* is pulling the boom downwards.

Similarly, in the case of a triangular sail, the head and clew will be under very high tension, which is distributed into the body of the sail. The foot and luff will experience high loadings, but this will be the case only if the sail is set up with high halyard loads and the foot is pulled tightly. Tension in these areas is lower than occurs in the leech, head and clew zones.

A more technological approach to determining the tensions in a sail lies in the use of load cells positioned at different points on the surface of the sail so that the direction and amount of tension can be established. The general trend is demonstrated in Fig 52 for a genoa. This *tension mapping* would apply regardless of the fabric employed, its thickness or its orientation. The mapping provides a graphic picture of how the sail needs to be built in order to keep stretch to a minimum, a figure of 1 per cent often being regarded as the upper limit.

in any direction. This would be the ultimate in structured fabrics and the sail would require little in the way of the adjustments described previously to ensure that its shape is maintained in a range of wind strengths. (More difficult, perhaps, would be adapting the shape to suit different winds since the sail would, in principle, be built for one condition only.)

For the sail to reach perfection it would need to be super-light, easy to stow and last for ever. It would of course need to be adequately strong (but not super-strong, which would be indicative of redundancy). Obtaining strength in a sail, whilst clearly necessary, is not the main focus of the sail-maker. More important is the assurance of low-stretch material oriented in a way that minimizes distortions so that the sail retains its built form.

Scotch-Cut
(Fig 53)

One of the earliest arrangements for sewing together the panels of a sail was the *scotch-cut,* otherwise known as the vertical or leech cut. Panels were arranged parallel to the leech. The warp threads dealt very successfully with the leech tensions.

Although regarded in its day as a successful sail type because the sail would still be usable if a seam failed, the contour of the sail as the air flowed over it would not have been fair because the double layer of cloth at the seams would have stretched less than the panels, resulting in an undulating surface. Another drawback was that a roach could not be exploited.

Cross-Cut
(Fig 54)

The *cross-cut* style of sail, still used today, possesses opposite characteristics to the scotch-cut sail. Panels are laid perpendicularly to the leech, enabling a roach to be included. Loadings in the leech place the weft threads in tension. A disadvantage with this cut is that, especially in the case of a mainsail, the roach results in bias in the cloth at the edge of the sail and therefore the cross-cut sail is prone to distortion, particularly where conventional fabrics of relatively low stability are used. Cross-cut spinnakers were used commonly in the 1960s and early 1970s, and the edge distortions are very apparent because of the inherent instability of the nylon fabric used for spinnakers.

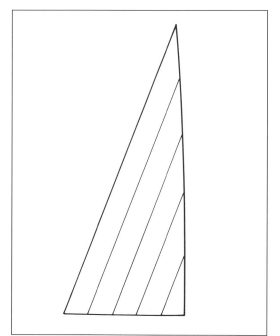

Fig 53   Scotch-cut.

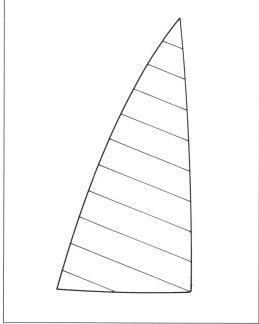

Fig 54   Cross-cut.

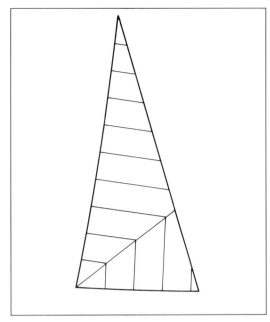

Fig 55   Mitre-cut.

Mitre-Cut
(Fig 55)

A variant of the cross-cut, and used principally for foresails, is the *mitre-cut*. It is claimed to possess great durability and strength. Panels are arranged so that they approach both leech and foot at right angles. Neither is liable to stretch because cloth bias at the edge is avoided.

The panel arrangement results in a seam, looking like a mitred joint, which runs diagonally from the clew. The mitre-cut is little used today and the level of protection to avoid foot stretch may be excessive with the improved cloths available, but the cut does allow for the consequent water loadings from waves breaking over the bow.

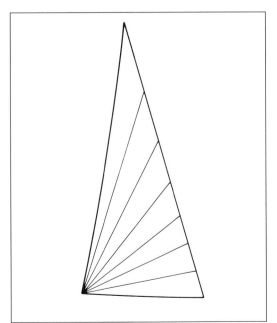

Fig 56   Radial-cut.

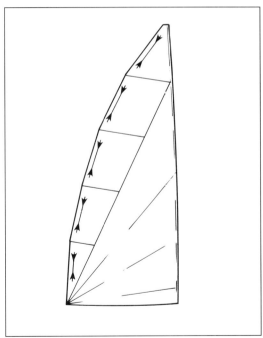

Fig 57   Cloth orientation in the roach for a sail of radial cut.

Radial-Cut
(Figs 56 & 57)

The use of *radial-cut* sails presented the beginning of a major step forward. Apparently invented and registered in America in 1869, the radial-cut sail more obviously deals with leech tension and clew loadings. In the early 1960s, Anderson Aerosails, a small English sail loft in Lancing, Sussex, specialized in radial sails that effectively dealt with the tensions occurring in the roach of a mainsail. The loft used separate panels between each of the battens and oriented the warp of the cloth to lie along the edge of the sail between each batten. The leech thus formed was not a fair curve but a series of straight lines between battens.

Normally, less stretch occurs in the weft of sail-cloth than in the warp because of the crimp, as described in Chapter 2. It is desirable that, for building radial sails, the cloth is manufactured with crimp in the weft, rather than the warp. Certainly, panel orientation is complex and expensive because the panels are not parallel, nor of the same

Fig 59   A somewhat stretched genoa leech. The leech line, used to prevent flutter, has been tightened to a minimum.

width as the cloth. Also, there may be a difference in bias as adjacent panels join at a seam, and this tends to result in differential stretch.

Leech Treatment
(Figs 58–61)

In order to avoid the *cupping,* or curling, which tends to be caused by a heavy fold of cloth called the *tabling,* usually used for reinforcing the leech, Anderson Aerosails used the woven edge of the sail-cloth, the *selvedge*, at the leech. Although most sail-makers would blanch at the thought, such a leech proved surprisingly resistant to stretch. The loft used the same

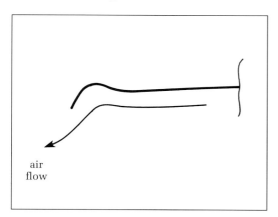

air
flow

Fig 58   The tabling stretches less than the cloth adjacent to the leech, producing a cupping effect.

Fig 60   The leech line has been over-tensioned.

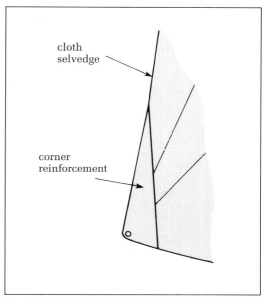

Fig 61   Hollow created in a foresail leech whilst maintaining the selvedge.

principle for the design of its foresails. Hollow in the leech was achieved by insetting the selvedge from the head and clew corner reinforcements, a straight line being formed between these points. It was my experience that the leeches of these genoas fluttered, but not enough to cause the whole genoa to vibrate and disturb the flow, as occurs with some foresail leeches even with a *leech line* used to tension the leech.

Semi-Radial Cut
(Fig 62)

Anderson Aerosails went on to develop the cut to a *semi-radial* design so that bias on the luff was more consistent. This enabled the luff to be tensioned to vary the position of maximum camber very readily, but with less differential of bias stretch that occurs with the radial design.

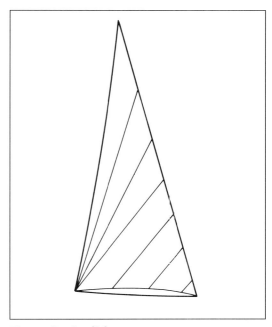

Fig 62   Semi-radial cut.

Fig 63 Radial-head spinnaker in use.

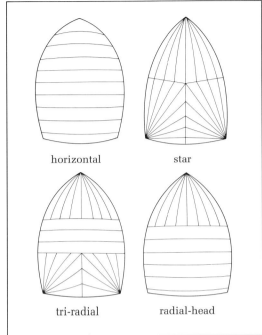

Fig 64 Common panel layouts for spinnakers.

Spinnaker Development
(Figs 63 & 64)

Despite the complexity of radial cuts, warp orientation is here to stay. The spinnaker descriptively termed *star-cut,* devised by sail-maker Bruce Banks, started a trend in spinnaker design that has never been reversed. The loadings occurring in all three corners were distributed as for the clew in radial fore-and-aft sails and this spinnaker proved very effective for reaching.

Developed from the star-cut, the ubiquitous *tri-radial* incorporates a centre section of horizontal panels to help the sail spread under load so that it satisfies the requirements both of downwind sailing and reaching. The tri-radial spinnaker deals with corner loadings so much better than the *horizontal-cut* spinnaker that the latter is rarely made today, despite the lower cost. The compromise *radial-head* spinnaker, whilst suitable for downwind sailing, probably has no place in a small sail wardrobe.

Recent developments have lead to full-radial spinnakers not totally unlike the star-cut spinnaker. Great attention has been given to tension mapping and the continuity of reinforcement.

Reinforcement Orientation

The use of film laminates has taken the principle of thread-line orientation much further. The orientation of the cloth or fibre reinforcement in a laminated sail follows more closely the tensions radiating from the corners into the body of the sail, as indicated by the tension mapping shown earlier in Fig 52. Applying this principle, some sails have appeared with very exotic cuts. Since, with laminated sails, reinforcement can be placed where it is wanted, the limitation imposed by cutting panels from bolts of cloth, resulting in linear reinforcement, has disappeared.

As a result, reinforcement can follow the lines of tension, which tend to adopt curves as they spread. This also ensures that transitions in the sail from low to high flexibility are smooth, thereby minimizing hard spots that disrupt the smooth curves of the sail. Curved reinforcement has the same effect as a hollow leech. Sheet tension results in a reduction in camber as the reinforcement straightens, but in this case there is no loss of area.

Building in Stiffness

The use of laminates enables stiffness to be built into a sail, such as is needed where an extended roach is employed in a mainsail but batten lengths are limited (for example, by class rules). Extra layers of fabric may be employed in such areas to provide a plated effect.

As a general rule, and without resorting to special reinforcements, the roach of a mainsail may be extended in the vicinity of a batten by about one third (though one half may be feasible) of the length of the batten. This principle applies to 'soft' sails, in which the battens are not the full width of the sail. If this proportion is exceeded, the roach is unlikely to stand successfully and is liable to create creases around the inboard ends of the battens.

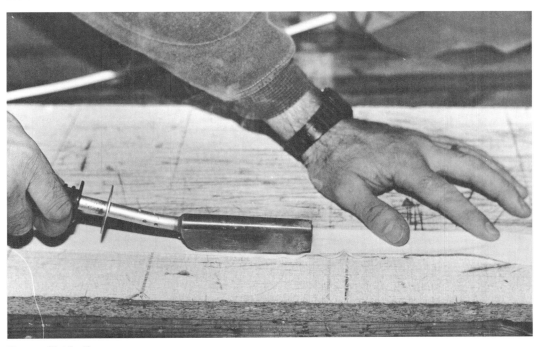

Fig 65   Hot knife.

Fig 66 Conventional zigzag and 5-step zigzag stitches, the latter providing additional strength.

Fig 67 Machine stitching. The sail-maker sits in a well so that the sail is at floor level for ease of manipulation.

Sometimes, short battens are fitted to the leech of short-footed jibs that overlap the mast by a small amount only. Battens in genoas are impractical because of the likelihood of snagging when turning through the wind.

Sail-Making Processes
(Fig 65)

The fundamental outline processes of sail-making bear description, the principal context described being for conventional polyester woven cloth sails, made conventionally. Once the design and cut of the sail are finalized, an outline is drawn on the loft floor. Cloth is rolled out and marked from the outline, and cut oversize with scissors.

If seams are to be formed using the selvedge of the cloth, each panel is overlapped by the seam width, which is often marked by a line one seam width in from the selvedge. In the case of seams not on the selvedge, for example where broadseaming or radial panels are employed, the shape of the panel is marked out and cut using a *hot knife* – rather like a soldering iron with a long cutting edge.

Seaming
(Figs 66 & 67)

The seams may be marked with adjacent pencil ticks in order to ensure that alignment is maintained when stitching together on the sewing machine. Because of the slippery nature of the cloth, it is helpful initially to glue the seams together, making the sewing process less arduous. Double-sided tape can be used as an alternative. Both edges of the seam are machine sewn using a zigzag stitch, which has a desirable yielding quality.

Thread of a different colour from that of the sail-cloth is often advocated so that broken threads can be spotted easily. Thread used for seaming is vulnerable, particularly on hard cloths, because it does not 'bed in' readily. Some people prefer white thread regardless. In order to protect the stitching, proprietary sealer can be applied when the sail is complete.

The Edges

The periphery of the sail is trimmed, allowing for the folding over and stitching of a tabling or the addition of a tape. A luff tape encasing a cord or rope may be fitted to reinforce the luff and ensure it 'returns' when the halyard is eased. Where appropriate, this would be designed for the mast or forestay luff groove, *sail slides* or foresail *hanks*. Flexible rigging wire is usually sewn into the luff of a dinghy foresail.

Corner Reinforcement
(Fig 68)

Each corner of the sail is reinforced with a number of layers of cloth, usually of the same type used for the body of the sail. These *patches* are arranged so that they complement the sail-cloth and provide progressive reinforcement. This is achieved by sewing on several progressively larger patches.

A small sail might have three patches sewn in, whilst the reinforcement of a large sail might be 12mm (1/2in) thick, clearly outside the scope of a domestic sewing machine. The head patches of a mainsail normally incorporate a headboard shaped from a solid material such as aluminium alloy, in order to cope with the extreme loadings to which this region of the sail is subjected.

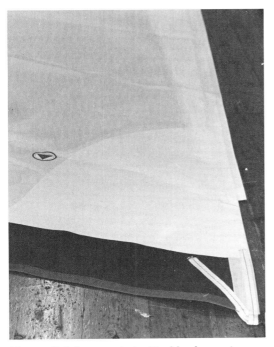

Fig 68 Reinforcement at critical load areas is provided by patches.

Fig 69 The components for four sizes of eye. The cutter is used on the sail-cloth and is matched to the largest eye shown.

Fig 70   Eye press.

Fig 71   Sail clew built with a ring and webbing rather than an eye, for high strength.

Finishing
(Figs 69–72)

The finishing stages of the sail-making process involve sewing in batten pockets, foresail hanks and reef points if required. *Eyes* are formed at each corner where halyard, clew outhaul or sheet and tack fixings will be attached. Traditionally, an eye comprises a brass ring sewn in position into which a brass turnover is punched to protect the stitching. In order to reduce the time taken to form a hand-worked eye, the technique has been superseded by eyes that are just punched in position.

Where appropriate, the final stages involve the sticking or sewing of the sail insignia and numbers, draft stripes (which provide an indication of sail camber), reef points and other details.

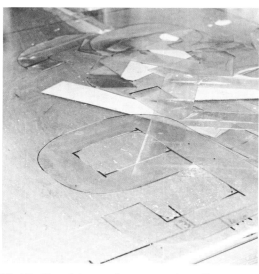

Fig 72   Templates used to cut out the sail insignia and numbers.

Technological Development

Advances in technology have led to an improvement in the quality of sails. Computer software is available that is able to make predictions based upon data specifying the desired shape, describe the shape of the panels needed to achieve this, propose a suitable cloth arrangement based upon the tension mapping and finally cut out the cloth.

To some extent, the process can be self-learning. The sail that works well can be replicated so that following sails also work well, and indeed such technological advances provide the capability of producing large numbers of ostensibly identical sails. Economy of scale is feasible and it is true to say that sails are relatively cheaper now than in the past.

Of course, such technological developments are extremely expensive and only the larger sail lofts are able to follow this path. Perhaps it is just a little worrying that we push buttons and the computer comes up with jelly-mould answers. Who knows, perhaps there are other possible sail shapes that would perform well or better. Perhaps there is a place yet for the small sail loft and the art of sail-making.

Taken to its extreme, the business of sail-making could become the inputting of data relating to the customer's requirements, carrying out instructions given by the computer and then assembling those parts that cannot be achieved robotically. But it is unlikely that the industry could ever be so large as to warrant such investment.

Summary

- Camber in a sail is achieved by cutting it so that it has luff round and by broad-seaming, and, when sailing, by sheeting or outhaul adjustments.

- The effect of the wind tends to induce excessive camber by fabric stretch and, in the case of the foresail, by luff sag. This is compensated for by systems for control of the foresail, such as the use of a hollow leech in conjunction with sheet tension and a tight forestay.

- An awareness of tension mappings enables sails to be built so that stretch is minimized. A variety of sail cuts has been developed, including the radial-cut, to provide appropriate reinforcement orientation.

- The process of making sails involves seaming, dealing with the edges of the sail, incorporating patches, making eyes and finishing. Computer software can deal with the sail design and the cutting of the cloth towards a reproducible product.

4
MATERIALS FOR MASTING AND RIGGING

Materials for Masts
(Fig 73)

Loaded as a strut, compression in the stayed mast results, in the extreme, in buckling. Significant bend leads to the mast's falling out of *column*, which precipitates failure.

In order to resist failure, the most significant property required of the constructional material is a resistance to deformation, or *stiffness*. Most pertinent is stiffness for weight (or stiffness for *density*, which is the mass per unit volume).

Material Stiffness and Strength

Wood is not as stiff as aluminium alloy. This can be verified by bending samples of the same section across your knee, or more scientifically by hanging weights on each sample and measuring the deflection for each.

The ratio of stiffness to density is quite similar for many common structural materials. This implies that a material that is five time as dense as another (the

approximate difference between aluminium alloy and wood) will be five times as stiff.

Using a material of high strength for a mast is also advantageous because it means that the mast will take on a more extreme bend before it finally buckles. Nevertheless, since the compressive load

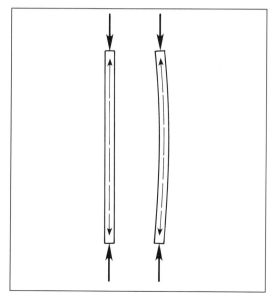

Fig 73   A representation of a mast in column (left) and out of column (right).

52

the mast is able to withstand decreases as bend increases, stiffness remains the principal virtue required of the mast material.

This demand does not contradict the need to produce deliberate mast bend in order to flatten the mainsail. A stiff mast material would enable a smaller section and hence lighter mast to be used so that it could be bent readily but remain resistant to collapse.

The achievement of especially high material stiffness for density requires the use of *exotic materials*, carbon fibre reinforced resin (usually epoxy) being one such. Similarly, increased strength for density is available from the exotics and the metallic materials can be enhanced for high strength.

Wood
(Figs 74 & 75)

Tall, straight-grained fir trees, free from branches and hence knots in the lower trunk, produce the best wooden spars. Generally, spars are hollowed over most of their length but left solid for significant fittings or attachment points, such as for the shrouds and spreaders. Structurally, this is efficient because it allows material to be removed where it is not required. Another advantage is that halyards produce less noise when they frap against a wooden mast than when they clang against a metal one.

The system by which the mast is shaped externally to a desirable section and hollowed internally in restricted areas only is labour intensive. By contrast, box-sectioned wooden masts constructed from four long planks are economical to build, if crude in section. Reinforcement in necessary areas can be accomplished by adding fillers of the same timber.

A sensible compromise between economics, weight and form is the circular mast constructed from a number of planks. These can be shaped using a spindle moulder so that effective joints are produced that provide relatively easy assembly.

The first hollow masts were built using

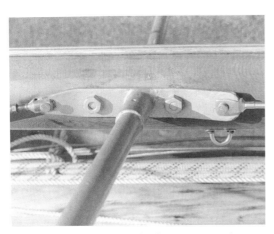

Fig 74   A wooden mast. The fittings are a mix of the old and the new.

Fig 75   Part of the end view of a jointed circular mast before finishing.

casein-based glue. These adhesives are derived from milk and can degrade if not protected by varnish, the generally preferred finish for wooden spars. The use of resin adhesives, introduced in the middle of the twentieth century, provides a more waterproof joint that is almost invariably stronger than wood when bonded along the grain.

The preference for varnishing wooden spars presents an aesthetic limitation to the adhesives used. Resorcinol formaldehyde, used extensively as the fully waterproof adhesive for boat-building, is dark brown in colour and consequently is avoided despite its superiority. A variant, urea formaldehyde, is somewhat less waterproof but because of its transparency is highly favoured, it being reasoned that spars are not subjected to continuous immersion. Another alternative is the use of epoxy adhesive, but some forms may darken with exposure to light more than the wood itself.

Metals

No other mast material can be shaped so readily as wood, and the use of aluminium alloy requires sophisticated techniques to produce mast taper or provide additional strengthening in some areas. This can never emulate the structural continuity obtained with the wooden mast. Nevertheless, aluminium alloy is a very suitable material, the wall thickness obtained being adequate to prevent localized denting but sufficiently thin to make the best of the section in resisting bending. The use of especially thick walls results in masts that are heavy for their resistance to bending.

Masts constructed from steel or stainless steel, by contrast, can have a much thinner wall for strength and weight compared with aluminium alloy, but the wall thickness, perhaps as little as 1mm for a small yacht, would prove inadequate against point loadings, though detailed reinforcement could overcome this.

Although high-specification steel tubes of 1mm and even 0.5mm wall thickness are successful on racing bicycles, the stability of such a thin-walled tube at a diameter of 26mm (1in) clearly will be greater than that for a 150mm (6in) diameter mast.

The low density of another metal, titanium, together with its superior strength and stiffness characteristics in comparison with aluminium alloy, presents a sensible if expensive route for masting boats. But probably the most serious contender for superior spars in the future lies with non-metallic materials.

Carbon Fibre

Although carbon fibre reinforced resin has an appropriate application for unstayed masts because the material presents an obvious means of significant weight reduction, its use for stayed masts is increasing and could become a much more prominent sector in the near future. Cost and the difficulties of manufacture weigh against carbon fibre, but both drawbacks are being overcome.

Because the material is available in fabrics of various orientations as is true for sail-cloth, reinforcement can be arranged for best effect. Resistance to bending is paramount for both unstayed and stayed masts, but torsional stiffness is also of some importance for the stayed mast because of the twisting effect of the spreaders.

In principle, fibre reinforcement offers

the means for dealing with these requirements. In contrast, aluminium alloy, the main material for mast construction, cannot offer these directional properties in the same way.

Aluminium Alloy

In reality, the aluminium alloy used for mast manufacture is not particularly plain or ordinary. Using pure aluminium would prove unsatisfactory because the mast would acquire a permanent set under relatively low loadings. The material is simply not strong enough.

The incorporation of small amounts of elements *alloyed* to the aluminium, together with *heat treatment*, improves the mechanical properties. Technological care needs to be taken to avoid proneness to fatigue, which results from cyclical loadings including vibration, and to corrosion. Whilst it is possible to produce mechanically superior aluminium alloys so strong that they cannot be bent to produce a set but break instead, some of the negative aspects already mentioned are unavoidable.

Generally, a compromise is sought. Aluminium alloys from the 6000 series, which describes its specification, are normally used but occasionally those from the 7000 series are employed for particular race applications. Low-quality spars can be made using grade 6063 alloy, whilst the norm is either 6061 or 6082.

Extrusions

High-grade alloys are more difficult to *extrude*, the process whereby the tube is manufactured. This process involves pushing a semi-molten billet of the alloy through a die or former of the same shape as the mast section. The extrusion produced may not be to the finished section. For efficient manufacture, the luff groove gap of a dinghy mast can be extruded oversized and mechanically closed to the correct gap afterwards.

The mast manufacturer is not directly involved with the production of the extrusions, but may own the various dies necessary for the range of spars offered.

Corrosion of the Mast
(Fig 76)

Masts are vulnerable to deterioration no matter from what material they are

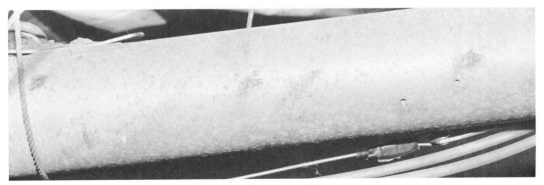

Fig 76   Corrosion occurring on a non-anodized aluminium alloy mast.

constructed. Surprisingly, carbon fibre cannot be excluded despite its apparent inertness. Most steels, as we all know, are prone to corrosion. Aluminium alloy represents a material that is suitable for mast manufacture, not only because of its good structural properties, but also because, with appropriate choice of alloying elements, it is resistant to corrosion.

Galvanic Corrosion

A common source of corrosion is where fittings are attached to masts by fastenings such as self-tapping screws. The dissimilarity in material of the screw and the mast wall results in *galvanic corrosion* in which an electrolytic cell is formed by water, especially when salty. The cutting of the thread also produces material changes in the aluminium alloy, further hastening corrosion.

The simplest solution is to limit direct contact between the metals. In the case of a self-tapping screw this involves driving in the screw, withdrawing it to apply a protective medium, then re-inserting. Generally, zinc chromate paste is used for such protection and would be applied to the contact surface of fittings as well as the fastenings. An alternative in the case of fittings is the use of an inert material, such as plastic, between the fitting and the mast.

Clearly, the use of similar metals in contact reduces the possibilities and extent of corrosion. It is often argued that aluminium pop rivets should be used in preference to stainless steel or Monel metal, despite the strength disadvantage.

However, Monel metal is commonly used. Because of the relative *nobilities* of the metals, Monel will lead to corrosion

in the aluminium. But the use of a small fastening in a relatively large mast offsets the effect. An aluminium fastening in a Monel metal mast would result in very much more rapid corrosion, again of the aluminium.

Because the aluminium from which the mast is extruded includes alloying elements to improve its structural properties, the differences in the materials of composition of the mast itself produce small galvanic cells, which means that the mast surface is vulnerable to corrosion. Although the resulting level of corrosion is not usually serious, nor does it detract significantly from the strength of the extrusion, the white powder produced can be unsightly.

Surface Protection

The classic procedure whereby corrosion of the mast can be eliminated is by *anodizing* during production. This process is electrochemical, rather like nickel plating, and artificially produces an oxide layer on the surface some 25 microns thick (about the thickness of very thin paper). A bonus in the process is that all exposed surfaces are anodized, which protects the inside of the mast as well as the outside.

The oxide layer can be dyed a variety of colours, but silver, black and gold are the most common. Silver is probably the most aesthetically pleasing, particularly as scratches on the surface through to the aluminium alloy are least obvious. However, the oxide layer is very hard and much more resistant to scratching than the alloy itself.

As an alternative to anodizing, masts can be painted. Although a wide range of paints could be used over an appropriate primer that etches the surface, probably the most suitable is a two-component polyurethane coating. When the components are mixed together, the polyurethane cures in a similar fashion to other synthetic resins, producing a hard, durable, long-lasting surface. The hardness of polyurethanes can be their undoing because, if the coating is moderately thick, it tends to chip easily. Whilst the use of conventional paints may seem a reasonable alternative, they need re-coating at much more frequent intervals.

Powder coating presents perhaps the best alternative to polyurethane paint. The plastic powder is sprayed onto the surface and fused by heating the mast extrusion to produce a continuous, resilient surface. The plastic flows readily to fill minor irregularities and its only drawback is that it is visually uninspiring.

Any surface coating, including anodizing, must be carried out when all work to the extrusion is completed, including welding. Sometimes, spreader brackets and other fittings are welded into place and masts are normally tapered by cutting out a long V shape in the extrusion and welding the edges together.

Because of the heat involved in the welding process, the mechanical properties of the aluminium alloy may be reduced (depending upon the grade of alloy used). Some alloys require further heat treatment after welding, involving the re-heating of the alloy to an appropriate temperature, followed by rapid cooling. Nevertheless, techniques of chemical welding and fabricating inside the mast tube overcome many difficulties associated with the use of extrusions.

Materials for Rigging

The diameter of standing rigging wire used for stayed masts depends upon the rigging layout and the boat's stability. Although adequate strength is required, a consideration for racing yachts in particular is minimizing the elasticity of the rig. Meeting this requirement may mean that the wire is somewhat over-strong. Cruising people would not complain about this.

Typical standing rigging diameters for an *aft-swept* single-spreader, three-quarter rigged, modern performance yacht of 7.5m (25ft) with ballast keel and basic cruising interior would typically be 5mm for the cap shrouds, lower shrouds and forestay; and 4mm for the backstay.

Wire Types

The sizes quoted are in 1 × 19 stainless steel wire (the wire comprises one bundle of nineteen strands). This type of wire is a standard for most sailing craft, whether dinghy or cruising or racing yacht. For more specialized racing craft, the use of wire of different materials enables smaller diameters to be used and in some cases results in less weight aloft.

Dyform wire, which utilizes stainless steel strands formed so that they pack fairly closely together, achieves a smaller diameter than is obtained with 1 × 19 wire for the same strength. The next step in refinement and cost is rod rigging, which could be described as 1 × 1. Because the section is solid and the rod is manufactured using materials of higher mechanical properties than stainless steel, such as Nitronic 50 or Cobalt MP 35 N, further reductions are possible in diameter and therefore in weight.

Further still, rigging 'wire' has been constructed from both carbon fibre and aramid fibre, with huge potential in terms of weight saving. High modulus polyethylene presents another possibility. The drawback is that windage is increased with these materials because the rod is of greater diameter than for the metallic materials, since the high-strength metals are stronger even than carbon fibre.

Fatigue
(Fig 77)

Another drawback with the use of carbon fibre in particular is that it tends towards brittleness and can tolerate little deformation, bending, vibration or impact before failure occurs. High-strength metal rod rigging suffers similarly.

In fact, stainless steel is not totally free from such problems, though the

flexibility conferred by 1 × 19 helps significantly. Some cruising sailors prefer 7 × 7 construction for greater flexibility still, whilst the use of galvanized steel, which is very resistant to fatigue, is preferred for long-distance cruising.

Nominal diameter (mm)	Tensile strength (kN)
2	3.1
3	7.0
4	12.5
5	19.6
6	28.2
7	34.7
8	45.4
9	57.5
10	71.0
26	397.4

Table 1. Tensile strength of 1 × 19 stainless steel wire. Larger diameters of wire are available up to 44mm. The breaking strengths are expressed in kN (kiloNewtons) and can be converted approximately to tons by dividing by ten.

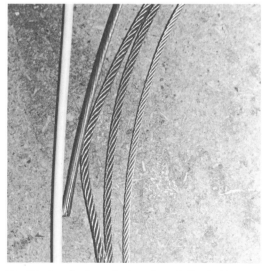

Fig 77   A selection of wires, from left: plastic coated stainless steel (for guard-rails); 1 × 19 stainless steel; 7 × 19 stainless steel; 7 × 7 stainless steel; 7 × 19 galvanized steel.

Rigging material and construction	Tensile strength (kN)	Weight (N/m)
1 × 19 stainless steel	28.2	1.73
7 × 7 stainless steel	23.1	1.52
1 × 19 Dyform	34.7	1.90
Nitronic 50 rod (22-13-5)	38.3	2.16
Titanium rod (6AL 4V)	25.4	1.23
Cobalt rod	46.8	2.33
Carbon rod	46.8	0.33
Kevlar rod	12.2	0.31
7 × 7 galvanized steel	25.1	1.31

Table 2. Comparative strengths and weights per metre for different rigging materials, each of 6mm diameter.

Strength

High-strength 1 × 19 stainless steel (of specification 316531) exhibits the tensile strengths shown in Table 1. Comparative strengths and weights for different rigging materials are shown in Table 2. The low-stretch characteristic of wire rope is exploited for halyards. A more flexible form is required in comparison with standing rigging because the halyards must bend around *sheaves* (the rollers over which the ropes run) so that sails can be hoisted from deck level.

Generally, wire rope of 7 × 19 construction in stainless steel or galvanized steel is favoured. Despite its tendency to rust, many people prefer galvanized steel rope because it is more resilient, does not work harden to the same degree and is less prone to stray wires breaking and escaping from the bundle.

Although 7 × 19 stainless steel wire rope is not super-strong (it is about 25 per cent weaker than 1 × 19 stainless steel), this is not of great importance, the main criterion being that of low stretch so that the sails remain close to their hoisted position. The use of polyester rope fails to meet this criterion, though stretch in spinnaker halyards is not so critical.

By contrast, modern aramid fibre and high modulus polyethylene ropes compare favourably with wire rope in terms of low-stretch properties, albeit with some increase in diameter. Aramid fibre does not tolerate well the severe bending resulting from the rope passing over sheaves and, as a result, the material has largely been superseded by HMPE. Both offer a significant reduction in weight over wire rope.

For running rigging, where low stretch is especially beneficial, such as for the spinnaker *guy* that holds the tack of the spinnaker and the pole in place, such ropes represent a major advance. No doubt, ropes will be developed in the future with lower stretch characteristics still. I should like to invent a rope that shortens as the load is increased to accompany my fanciful suggestion for a sail-cloth that contracts as the wind gusts in order to reduce camber.

SUMMARY

- In order that a mast may stay reasonably in column, the material of construction requires the property of stiffness that lends resistance to bending. Strength in the material also is necessary so that failure when the mast is bent does not occur.

- Masts in wood can be shaped and hollowed readily. The tapering of aluminium alloy extrusions involves welding, which demands re-heat treatment in the case of high-strength alloys. Carbon fibre reinforced resin represents a high-performance alternative material.

- Aluminium alloy of the grades used for masts are corrosion resistant, but anodizing, painting and powder coating nullify the problem. Fittings and fastenings should be separated from the aluminium alloy in order to avoid galvanic corrosion.

- Stainless steel of 1 × 19 construction is used ubiquitously for standing rigging, with Dyform and rods in various high-strength materials available for performance purposes. Galvanized steel presents an alternative that is less prone to brittleness and fatigue, and, along with low-stretch fibre ropes, can be used for halyards.

5
MAST AND
RIGGING DECISIONS

Choosing the Mast Section
(Fig 78)

The requirements for the mast of a dinghy or racing yacht tend to be low weight, adequate strength, low windage and controllable bending characteristics. The elements of weight, strength and windage in some respects are contradictory, whilst the aspect of bending relates more to the rigging configuration than the mast itself if the section is not very large.

For an aluminium alloy mast of tubular construction, a section of small diameter with a thick wall could be of equal strength to a tube of large diameter with a thin wall. From the point of view of the flow of the air past the mast, the smaller-sectioned mast is superior: the drag and air disturbance over the mainsail are less. However, the heavy mast, which results from using a thick-walled small section, reduces the boat's stability. Weight aloft raises the overall centre of gravity, leading to increased heel.

When sailing upwind in a seaway, yachts tend to hobby horse or *pitch* because of oncoming seas, which disrupts the air flow in the sails. Weight in the mast exaggerates this effect just as weight in the bow particularly (but also the stern) tends to perpetuate pitching. Although weight displaced from the centre either

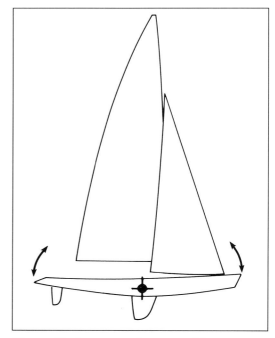

Fig 78   The boat responds to waves like a see-saw pivoted about a point, although experience indicates that the pitch centre may be further aft than shown.

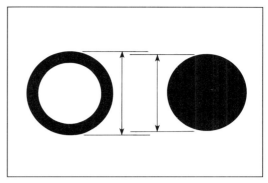

Fig 80   Two theoretical mast sections equal in structural capability, slightly different in terms of windage and very different in terms of weight.

Fig 79   A classic boat, replete with *baggywrinkle* for sail protection, suffers a high windage penalty.

horizontally or vertically results in resistance to starting pitching, once started it becomes difficult to stop.

Rigging Windage
(Fig 79)

The weight-versus-windage debate extends to the rigging. Multitudinous rigging, having significant windage in itself, permits a lightweight and low-windage mast and, conversely, a minimalist rigging layout demands a more bulky mast. Although reasonable solutions have been found, the various arrangements of rigging, mast diameter and wall thickness imply that no final answer has been determined.

For a cruising yacht, the decision is relatively easy to make. Cruising folk are not averse to a little bit of weight, or windage for that matter. They like the combination of belt and braces.

Roll Response

From another point of view, weight in the rig can be beneficial. Just as weight aloft affects a yacht's pitch response, so the behaviour in *roll* caused by waves approaching from the side is modified. A heavy mast slows down the yacht's responsiveness to waves, leading to a much slower motion. This is regarded as more comfortable.

The reduction in stability from using a heavier mast for the cruising yacht can be compensated for easily enough at the design stage by increasing the weight of the ballast keel slightly. This would only be necessary to ensure that the yacht has adequate power to carry sail.

Heavy masts in practice reduce the likelihood of capsize because the yacht's roll response to waves is slowed, giving time for the wave to pass before the boat inverts. The yacht also benefits from adequate area in the keel's planform, or shape in profile. Wings on the keel further slow roll response. The damping effect from a large underwater area also limits the tendency of the heavy mast to perpetuate roll.

Structural Efficiency
(Fig 80)

Even for the cruiser, weight is best coupled with structural efficiency (good strength for weight). For the racing boat, structural efficiency is paramount. Fig 80 shows hypothetical sections for a solid and a hollowed mast drawn to scale. Both have the same resistance to failure but the solid mast weighs four times as much as the hollow mast.

The principle applies to any material; greater structural efficiency results if the mast has a thinner wall than indicated by Fig 80 and a slightly larger diameter. The use of aluminium alloy is an obvious choice.

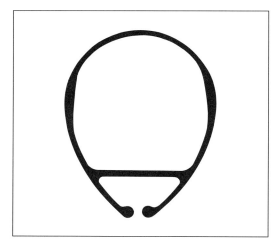

Fig 81   The section of a mast for a large dinghy. Although of relatively thin wall, local thickness is increased to produce greater transverse stiffness.

Mast Sections
(Fig 81)

Manufacturers of aluminium alloy masts embody this principle in mast production. Obviously, the range offered by manufacturers is limited, and mast design involves the selection of an extrusion that most closely meets the specification, with due regard given to a factor of safety. A manufacturer might choose a section rather larger than is strictly necessary.

Some companies list their sections using a numbering system based upon the external dimensions. Hence, a 6641 section would indicate an extrusion measuring 6.6in (168mm) by 4.1in (104mm). No clue is given about the shape of the section.

The external dimensions provide a means of assessing the resistance to bending of a mast built using this section of extrusion. For example, the mast would be expected to display more resistance to bending fore-and-aft than athwartships. Fig 81 shows a section suitable for a large dinghy, in which it can be seen that the side wall has been increased in thickness to provide increased transverse stiffness without an increase in the external dimensions.

Avoiding Local Stresses
(Fig 82)

Although longer lengths are possible, the practical production of extrusions limits the length to about 15m (50ft). This means that long aluminium masts must be joined. This may seem an undesirable practice, but the joint is usually stronger than the extrusion itself. Therefore it is

Fig 82   Joint on an aluminium alloy mast.

Fig 83   Reinforcement in the bottom part of a mast from a large racing yacht.

good practice to locate the joint, or joints if the mast is particularly tall, where extra strength is required, such as at the spreader positions.

Joints are created by butting the ends together and inserting a suitably shaped internal sleeve. If masts of a particular section are made infrequently, the sleeve might be produced using a short length of the mast extrusion itself that has been split and welded. Sleeves are normally bonded into position and mechanically fastened using pop rivets. The result is not especially pleasing to the eye but tends to get lost in the scale of a large yacht.

Weakening and Strengthening
(Fig 83)

An important principle for the mast builder is that holes should be staggered, rather than in neat rows. The pop rivet positions for the mast joints are arranged suitably, but, with twice the thickness of

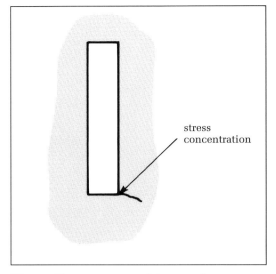

Fig 84   Sharp corners precipitate cracks.

Fig 85   Nicely rounded corners are featured in this mast opening.

material resulting from the sleeve plus extrusion, the problem is less acute than for the attachment of the various fittings at points of single thickness.

Because a large number of fittings are attached to the bottom of the mast and this area is vulnerable, the mast is often doubled in this region or deliberately reinforced using a substantial track for the spinnaker boom end fitting. Exits for the halyards, which normally run inside the mast, result in large openings in the bottom of the mast. Weakening is minimized not only by avoiding openings at the same height but also by ensuring that the cut-outs do not have square corners.

Stress Concentration
(Figs 84 & 85)

The use of rounded corners ensures that the loadings in the material itself, particularly tensile ones, are not focused at a sharp, internal corner that leads to high *stress*. Stress provides a measure of the amount of load in a structure relative to the area withstanding the load. In the vicinity of the corner, the area of aluminium under load is small, which indicates a *stress concentration.*

Stress concentrations precipitate cracks that then elongate and can lead to failure, particularly for high-strength materials that tend to be unyielding. Although the aluminium alloy from which masts are built is not of super-high strength, the avoidance of stress concentration is important, as failure can be catastrophic. Inspection also is difficult over most of the length of the mast.

A particular cause of stress concentration arises in the use of threaded fastenings. The profile of the thread in the mast produces sharp corners, although the problem is far less serious than for a hole with square corners in the mast wall. Nevertheless, self-tapping screws that cut their own thread are not strongly advised because they produce a particularly sharp thread in the aluminium alloy.

Air Past the Mast

Two reasons for tapering the topmast are to reduce weight and to improve bending characteristics. Another is to improve the air flow over the mast and hence over the top of the mainsail. As the sail narrows towards its head, efficiency is much reduced by mast interference; tapering the mast minimizes this effect.

Different Sections
(Figs 86 & 87)

Interference with the flow over the mainsail represents a greater loss than the windage of the mast section. The pear-shaped sections available may seem aerodynamic (and indeed they are when the wind approaches the boat and mast from ahead or at a small angle) but when the boat is sailing upwind, and certainly when on a reach, the profile presented is less attractive, assuming the mast is non-rotating.

Rectangular sections perform less well still. Greater hope lies with oval- and

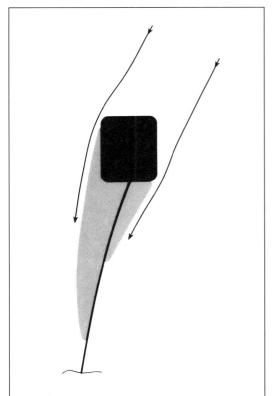

Fig 86 Rectangular sections produce significant disruption of air.

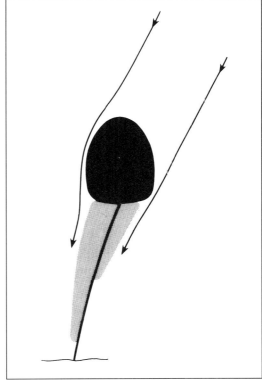

Fig 87 Delta sections may reduce turbulence as shown, but their greatest plus point is structural.

Fig 88   The use of mainsail slides normally results in a small space between the sail and the mast.

The interesting possibility for the delta-shaped section is that its corners may cause the air to divert towards the mainsail in the same way that turbulators change flow characteristics on golf and cricket balls. Nevertheless, such a possibility is dependent on air speed.

The principal reason for the spar-makers' use of delta- and oval-shaped sections relates to structural rather than aerodynamic gain. Both sections, and to an even greater extent the rectangular section, possess high resistance to bending. The delta section confers a particularly high transverse stiffness, which suits fractional rigs well.

Escaping Air
(Fig 88)

One aid to mast and mainsail aerodynamics is the use of a mainsail luff that attaches to the mast without a space through which air can pass from the high-pressure windward side to the low-pressure leeward side. This passage of air reduces mainsail efficiency because of the reduction of the air pressure differential responsible for the force produced by the sail.

Most efficient from this point of view is the use of a *bolt rope* – a rope attached to the luff of the mainsail that runs in a groove formed in the mast extrusion.

Sail Slides
(Fig 89)

The advantage of sail slides lies in the ease of handling. When the mainsail is lowered, the sail remains attached to the mast above the boom, whereas the bolt-rope system has no such means of retention, the sail then being loose on the

delta-shaped sections. It would be nice to think that the air flow over the delta shape, in particular, would be enhanced.

However, examination of the exposed area of the mast to the wind is not a realistic way of determining the interference with the mainsail. Rather, the air flow itself bears scrutiny. Theory suggests that the delta section could produce air flow that detracts less from the performance of the mainsail than do other types. Because we seek to improve the air flow in favour of the lee side of the mainsail, the mast section that enables the air to attach sooner to the mainsail on this side is likely to be the aerodynamic favourite, all other things being equal.

Fig 89   In a breeze, the mainsail can be recalcitrant.

Fig 90   Sleeved luff on a soft sail.

deck. The slides can be cumbersome to fit because they are fed onto the mast, starting with the head, before hoisting. A system known as a *pre-feeder* obviates this, the mainsail being fed from the bottom upwards into a separate section of mast track that feeds into the main section.

Sleeved Luffs
(Fig 90)

A convenience for sailing dinghies employing unstayed rigs is the use of *sleeved luffs*. The principle is a simple one: a sleeve is sewn into the sail so that it will slide over the mast before stepping. The use of full-length battens permits greater aerodynamic advantage, exploited most obviously in sailboard sails.

The battens are over-length so that they push positively against the mast and therefore tend to flop on one side or the other of the mast tube. Because of the effect of the wind, the battens take up a position on the lee side of the mast, rotating the sleeved luff with them.

Aerodynamically, this system has advantages over the conventional method of sail setting. Air flow is enhanced over the low-pressure, high-speed, leeward side of the sail, increasing the difference in pressure and therefore the force produced by the sail. It is true that flow over the windward side of the sail is worsened but this loss is outweighed. Such is the enthusiasm of sailboarders that this system has been dubbed the *rotating asymmetrical foil* (or RAF).

A further step for the sailboarders was

to extend the sleeved luff so that the deficiencies of the windward side of the mainsail could be overcome. In order to support the sleeve, moulded plastic *camber inducers* are employed. These rigid extensions of the battens fit onto the mast, permitting the battens to rotate as for the rotating asymmetrical foil.

Rotating Masts

An alternative means towards the same end is the one adopted mostly by multihulls. The high speed of multihulls means that the wind felt on board, known as the *apparent wind,* is higher than for slower-speed craft, particularly when sailing upwind. Efficiency of the rig therefore is crucial.

Sleeved luffs are not feasible because multihulls usually employ stayed rigs. Instead, the mast typically is of wing form and rotates so that it adopts a position whereby the lee side of the mast aligns with the lee side of the sail. Such masts are usually described as *over-rotating* and a spanner-like mechanism is used to control the angle of the mast to that of the sail.

One or two early dinghies adopted masts that rotated in line with the boom. With such a layout, little advantage is gained when sailing upwind because the boom is sheeted virtually on the centre-line and therefore the mast position is much the same as for a fixed mast. It is likely that there would be some small gain when sailing on a reach.

In order to permit masts that rotate to do so freely, the attachment of shrouds and stays must be at the front of the mast. Spreaders must also be able to rotate, but this reduces the degree of support they are able to provide to the mast. The better

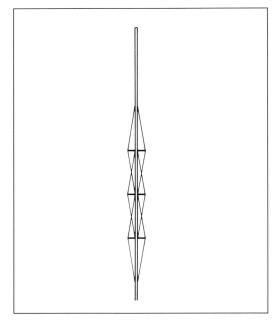

Fig 91 Multiple-diamond shrouds.

solution is to link both spreaders and then pivot at the front of the mast.

This rigging complication is avoided by the use of *diamond shrouds and struts* that then rotate with the mast. For multihulls, the *shroud base* is wide and spreaders from the mast to the shrouds would be unconventionally long. The use of bracing, self-contained on the mast as for diamond shrouds, presents a better solution.

Rigging Layouts
(Fig 91)

Some dinghies, such as the International 14 in the days of cotton sails, used an extensive multiple-diamond layout, even though the mast was non-rotating. It is probable that the windage produced was

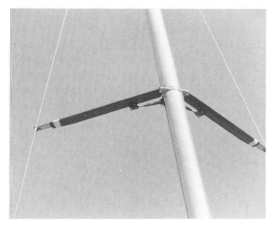

Fig 92   Fully adjustable dinghy spreaders.

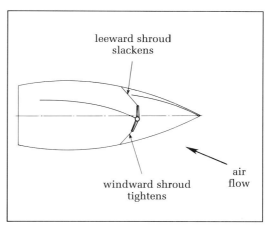

Fig 93   Limited control results if the shrouds are not pre-tensioned substantially.

greater than for a larger-sectioned mast with less rigging. Nevertheless, the mast is split into a large number of shorter panels, which is structurally efficient without producing cumulative compression towards the bottom of the mast, as is true for the normal yacht's rigging layout.

Diamond shrouds clearly limit the mast's transverse bend, but they do have an effect, albeit lesser, on fore-and-aft bending. As the mast bends, normally forward in the middle, the diamond struts pull the diamond shrouds forward. The diamond shrouds are therefore distorted from their line and in turn provide a limited degree of restraint. They must be in sufficient tension to produce this effect.

Fixed Spreaders
(Figs 92 & 93)

By far the most common rig arrangement for sailing dinghies involves fixed spreaders attached to a fixed rather than rotating mast. The spreaders push the shrouds outwards by a small amount. When sailing, the wind in the sails causes the windward shroud to tighten further and the leeward shroud to slacken. The windward spreader therefore prevents the middle of the mast bowing to windward, which is its natural tendency because of the unsupported topmast falling away to leeward.

Fore-and-aft support also is provided by the spreaders. As the mast bends, the spreaders pull the shrouds forward in a similar fashion to the diamond shrouds and struts. This pulls the shrouds from their line, restraining the mast, the force required being relatively small and within the realms of a push from a hand.

The system is fairly complex. In operation, the leeward shroud slackens when sailing upwind and allows the leeward spreader forward as the mast bows in the middle. Consequently, the effect is to twist the mast, which, because it lacks high torsional stiffness, lessens the degree of mast control.

Mast Inversion
(Fig 94)

In order to control mast bend, the spreaders are commonly angled slightly forward so that they have a tendency to pull the middle of the mast backwards. Such restraint presents the possibility of using a mast of lighter section, but when sailing downwind the restraint works against the mast. The drawback is that the mast may have a tendency when sailing downwind to invert – to bend so that its middle bows towards the stern as a result of the aftwards push by the spreaders. In this state, the mast is vulnerable to failure.

Good control is provided by support at the deck, which lowers the risk of mast inversion. Most dinghy masts are stepped at the keel and supported at the deck, often with a means for adjustment so that mast bend can be varied. Because of this level of bracing, which has an effect well above the deck, the spreaders can be placed above mid-shroud height, thus improving the overall level of control.

Yacht and Dinghy Rigging Compared
(Fig 95)

Although the principles of dinghy rigging apply to yachts, the rigging layouts are different. Weight aloft for a yacht is more critical than for a dinghy because of the heeling effect. Proportionally, a yacht's mast weight is less than that for a dinghy. This suggests the need for more extensive rigging. Also, the shroud base for yachts

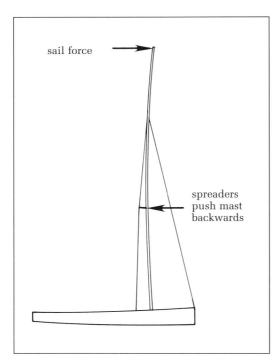

Fig 94   Mast inversion.

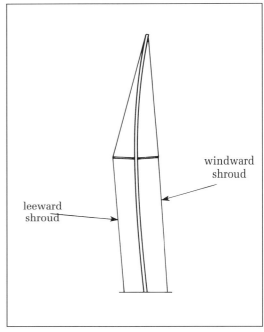

Fig 95   Long spreaders are not feasible without lower shrouds.

must be proportionally smaller so that the genoa can be sheeted at a smaller angle for close-windedness.

The narrow shroud base results in an insufficiently small *shroud angle* if no spreaders are used. This angle, at which the shrouds meet the mast, can be increased by the use of spreaders. A shroud angle of 11° is often regarded as the minimum, but new materials and technology have reduced this by a degree or two. Nevertheless, it is necessary for the spreaders to displace the shrouds by a significant amount when the shroud base is narrow.

Although the arrangement by which a mast is supported athwartships by only a pair of spreaders and shrouds (as for a dinghy) appears stable, it is not so when the spreaders are long. As one shroud tightens further and the other slackens when sailing upwind, the effect is that the tensioned shroud pushes harder on the spreader and the slack shroud reduces its associated spreader's push.

The effect is one of causing the mast to bow in the middle to leeward, that is sideways. The mast is unstable in this state. The thrust from the windward spreader is countered by employing a lower shroud that is adjusted when the rig is set up, so that the mast remains straight athwartships when under load.

Sometimes two lower shrouds are used on each side of the yacht and located on the deck fore and aft of the cap shroud. This arrangement provides fore-and-aft as well as athwartships support to the middle of the mast. Although fore-and-aft bending is restrained by the spreaders bearing on the shrouds, as is true for the dinghy rig, the use of shrouds in this way provides more positive support.

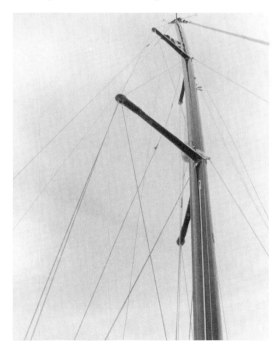

Fig 96   Aft-swept rig using additional diamonds for enhanced mast stability.

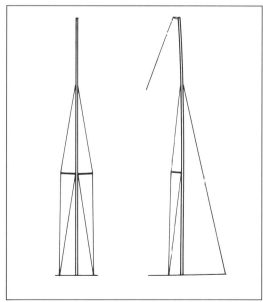

Fig 97   Aft-swept rig.

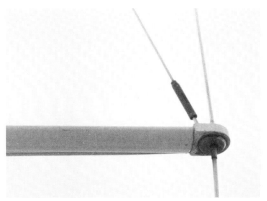

Fig 98   Cap and intermediate shrouds held captive by the spreader end cap.

Fig 99   Discontinuous rigging linked at the spreader end.

Additional Stays

Lower shrouds of this kind do restrict the full movement of both the main boom and spinnaker boom. This limitation is overcome by using checkstays (which prevent the mast from bowing forward and often are linked to the running backstays) and an inner forestay that restrains the mast in the other direction. None of these stays supplants the lower shrouds, which form part of the standing rigging.

A drawback to the use of such stays, like running backstays, is that they sometimes require release or adjustment whilst sailing. This is not particularly acceptable to cruising sailors, unless such running rigging provides additional support for use in extreme conditions and can be disconnected for normal sailing.

Aft-Swept Rig
(Figs 96 & 97)

An alternative system to overcome the use of running backstays, checkstays and inner forestay involves sweeping the spreaders aft. The cap and lower shrouds

are located at an appropriate position on the deck aft of the mast.

The result is a very stable system that controls the mast in all directions and resists the forestay loadings. However, the level of forestay tension that can be achieved is inferior to that provided by running backstays, and the shrouds and spreaders do affect the setting of the mainsail adversely when sailing downwind.

Multiple Spreaders
(Figs 98 & 99)

More complex rigging systems permit smaller mast sections to be employed by reducing the mast's panel lengths. This is achieved on sailing yachts by using two or more sets of spreaders. The arrangement of the shrouds is shown in Fig 13 in Chapter 1, from which it is seen that there are two vertical shrouds for the two-spreader rig depicted. It follows that four verticals are required for a four-spreader rig.

Since this arrangement is untidy and a producer of high windage, no-cost-spared racing yachts use discontinuous rigging. Links are involved at all spreader ends except for the top spreader. The diameter of the rigging is varied according to predicted loading and so, for example, the lowest vertical would have a single wire, equal in strength to the two verticals for the two-spreader rig or the four verticals for the four-spreader rig.

For single-spreader rigs it is well enough accepted that the spreader angle in the vertical plane should be such that the shroud angle is bisected. In this way, the spreader is least likely to be forced up or down at its end. A similar aim is sought for multiple-spreader rigs.

Forestay Tension

Tension in the shrouds needs to be fairly high to prevent the mast from falling off to leeward. For the fractionally rigged racing yacht's aft-swept rig without running backstays, the shroud tension needs to be as high as is tolerable in order to achieve acceptable forestay tension. Such extremes, however, can damage the yacht's structure, for example the attachment of the bulkhead to the hull in way of the mast.

For the masthead rig, the backstay acts directly on the forestay and at a sensible angle, achieving high forestay tension and minimizing foresail sag and its associated inefficiency. On a fractionally rigged yacht, the backstay tends to bend the mast rather than tension the forestay. The solution lies in the use of jumper stays, enabling the backstay load to be transmitted more effectively to the forestay.

Ending and Attaching the Wires

Ends must be formed in the standing rigging for attachment to the mast and deck, the type depending upon the diameter of the wire and its construction. At one time, the only system available was hand splicing in a similar fashion to the way in which an eye splice is formed in three-stranded fibre rope.

Swaged Eyes
(Figs 100 & 101)

For multi-stranded wire of small diameter, the swaging process has long

Fig 100   Talurit swaging machine.

Fig 101   Swages and two ferrules.

Fig 102 Norseman terminal system. The centre strands of the wire pass through the cone.

Fig 103 Making up a rolled swage wire terminal.

proved reliable. Using *swages* (dies formed to shape), a *ferrule* is squeezed around both the wire and the end after it has been turned round a *thimble* to form an eye. Ferrules made from copper are used for stainless steel wire, whilst aluminium ferrules are employed for galvanized steel. The difference in material is to minimize galvanic corrosion between the wire and the ferrule.

Both the copper and aluminium are in malleable form so that, when swaged, the ferrule is able to conform well to the wire, affording an excellent grip. The wire should fail under tension before pulling through the ferrule.

A weakness of the system is that failure of the wire is heightened where it emerges from the ferrule. Any bending of the wire relative to the ferrule results in a stress concentration in the corner, which precipitates failure. This area is vulnerable also because water tends to be trapped in it, leading to possible galvanic corrosion.

Generally, however, the swaging system is inexpensive, easy and quick, and do-it-yourself equipment is available.

This comprises swages that can be squeezed together using the same leverage system as that employed on bolt crops. Such ends can also be made using swages in a vice, although this is frowned upon because insufficient compression is achieved on wire of a modest diameter. The professional equipment for dinghy and small yacht rigging, which lends the trade names Talurit or Nicopress to the process, involves a hydraulic press with a high maximum load.

Swaging of this kind is not suitable for larger sizes of wire, particularly wire of 1 × 19 construction, which cannot bend to produce an eye without damage. Alternative connection methods also provide neater ends than those resulting from swaged eyes in large-diameter wire.

Norseman Terminals
(Fig 102)

The Norseman system provides a neat termination suited to 1 × 19 wire that is also very suitable for self-assembly either on or off the boat using a spanner. Wires can be formed to length and indeed shortened by re-making the *terminal*.

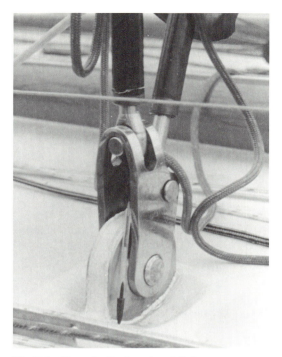

Fig 104 Shroud adjustment and fixings on a large yacht. Note the scale evidenced by the ball-point pen.

Each terminal comprises three parts that fit together to clamp the wire. A split cone and compression fittings screwed together clamp the centre strands to the outer strands, the friction preventing slippage. A non-corrosive marine sealant is applied to prevent the ingress of salt water.

Compact Ends
(Fig 103)

Perhaps the neatest end fittings involve the use of roll or rotary hammer swages. The fitting – be it eye or fork end or threaded bar – that forms one end of a *bottlescrew* finishes in tubular form. The internal diameter of the tube is the same

as the wire diameter and the fitting is swaged into the wire by the high force that the rolling or hammering provides.

Bottlescrews
(Figs 104 & 105)

Various fittings to attach the wires to the boat and to the mast are available. Bottlescrews of some kind are indispensable for adjusting the length of the rigging to achieve adequate tension. Usually, the bottlescrew comprises two threaded ends, one right-handed and one left-handed; the 'bottle' part joining the two ends can be rotated to effect the adjustment.

Bottlescrews are attached to the rigging on a more or less permanent basis and then connected, more or less temporarily, to a *chainplate* bolted to the hull. Alternatively, the bottlescrew can be

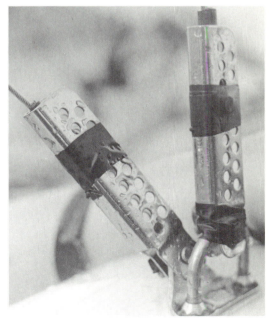

Fig 105 Adjuster plates.

Fig 106   Earlier system for attaching shrouds to the mast.

Fig 107   T-ball mast terminal with one style of retainer.

Fig 108   Toggle takes the form of a universal joint.

linked to some other fitting that bolts to the deck or a bulkhead where the shrouds are inboard.

Frequently, dinghies dispense with bottlescrews and rely upon adjuster plates for the shrouds which enable discrete adjustments to be made. The jib halyard is then tensioned using a lever, a screw adjuster or some other means which also tensions the shrouds.

Mast Attachments
(Figs 106–108)

Fittings to attach the wires to the mast have become quite sophisticated. One early system comprised a *tang* or plate to which an eye in the wire was connected by a shackle. This arrangement has been superseded by one in which the eye is attached to a pin, termed a *clevis* pin, through a pair of tangs on the mast.

In turn, this method has been surpassed by generally simpler systems having less windage. T-type terminals hook into a reinforced rectangular hole in the mast at 90 degrees to the final position and then are rotated to stop them from falling out. Retainers are available so that the accidental detachment of a wire when stepping the mast is avoided.

Ball types are also available, and these improve the freedom of articulation. Similarly, articulation needs to be built into the joints at deck level in order to avoid undue bending loads being applied to the wires or fittings. Forked fittings or toggles that permit freedom of movement in two directions meet the requirements well enough. These and other refinements to the masting and rigging have led to major improvements in reliability.

Summary

- The choice of mast section is a compromise between the conflicting requirements of low weight and low windage. High mast weight, within reason, is acceptable for cruising yachts since the roll response is slowed.

- Additional reinforcement, jointing and openings used in the building of masts should be structurally continuous in order to minimize stress concentrations.

- The achievement of satisfactory air flow past the mast requires an appropriate choice of section and a tapered topmast. The systems used for sailboards and multihulls present more aerodynamic solutions.

- Yachts require one or more sets of spreaders that displace the shrouds substantially in order that a narrow shroud base can be achieved. This demands additional shrouds to resist the thrust from the spreaders, unlike the much simpler dinghy layout.

- Rigging terminations, such as Talurit and roll swaging, Norseman, T- and ball-type terminals, have become progressively more reliable, neat and of low windage.

6

CONTROLLING
SPARS AND SAILS

Adjusting the Rigging

Once set up, the standing rigging is not adjusted as a rule whilst sailing. The same is not true of the running rigging, which is adjusted at intervals so that the mast can be bent and forestay tension attained.

By way of exception to the 'never touch the standing rigging' rule, sophisticated racing dinghies incorporate the means for fine adjustment to modify *rake*. This is used as a system for '*de-powering*' the rig, resulting in the reduction of heeling force, and can be carried out as an alternative or

Fig 109   Big boat hydraulics.

in addition to bending the mast. All this can be done from the trapeze.

Detachable Rigging

In order to permit the main boom and spinnaker pole a full range of movement, some wires, such as the inner forestay, are detachable. For small yachts, a *pelican hook*, which operates rather like an over-centre catch, enables speedy removal.

Backstay Adjustment
(Figs 109–111)

The running backstays and checkstays, which may be interconnected, often lead to winches or some other system, as they require frequent release and tightening and also scope for minor adjustment.

Also contrary to the standing rigging rule, and particularly for racing, tension is increased in the backstay for sailing upwind, in order to increase forestay tension or bend the mast to improve mainsail shape. Conversely, the backstay is slackened when sailing downwind.

Conventional bottlescrews would not provide a satisfactory system, though one early type of adjuster uses a bottlescrew to which a wheel is attached to provide adequate leverage. This type is best suited

Fig 110   Backstay tensioning device that is not very efficient because the pair of blocks does not return readily up the backstay splits when released.

Fig 111   Tackle attached to one split of a bifurcated backstay.

to masthead-rigged yachts, where relatively little adjustment is called for and where the loadings are high.

Better is a hydraulic adjuster – not unlike the hydraulic jack used to lift the corners or ends of cars. Hydraulic adjusters must be matched to the boat so that excessive backstay tension is avoided by setting the overload valve to an appropriate value.

At the other end of the cost scale, a pair of *blocks* pulled down a bifurcated (split) backstay has been used on smaller yachts, but this is not a good solution. The incorporation of a lever in the backstay, attached to a *tackle*, is more effective. A tackle, pronounced 'taykle', is a system of blocks (or pulleys) and line.

The backstays on fractionally rigged boats are relatively lightly loaded, but a large range of adjustment is required. Small yachts therefore often use direct tackles.

Systems for Mechanical Advantage

Most adjustments on dinghies and yachts need to be easy to achieve. Some forces are high, notably as boat size increases, and it is not feasible for the crew to make the changes called for directly to the spars and sails. Many systems offering

79

Fig 112   J-class style rigging.

mechanical advantage are employed to make tasks easier and in some cases permit fine, accurate adjustment.

One-Way Control
(Figs 112–114)

Large sails demand an effective means of control. By contrast, the relatively small foresail or spinnaker of a dinghy can be pulled in directly by the crew, though larger dinghies may have fitted a means whereby the foresail can be pulled in unaided but the sheet release is limited. An example of this is a *snubbing winch,* a drum around which the sheet is wound that rotates in one direction only. Friction of the rope on the drum permits the crew to hold the sheet with minimal force.

Fig 113   Ratchet block.

confusing for the inexperienced, who may expect to wind the sheet clockwise on one side and anti-clockwise on the other. As a result, handed winches have been fitted to some yachts.

Gearing Up

More sophisticated winches include gearing systems so that a single revolution of the winch handle produces one half or less of a revolution of the drum. This multiplies the leverage of the handle. The incorporation of a *self-tailing* system, which obviates the need to haul on the sheet whilst winding, further eases the task of foresail sheeting.

Fig 114   Ratchet blocks can include cam cleating.

A more sophisticated method involves the use of a *ratchet block,* sometimes used on *mainsheets* as well. Some ratchet blocks rotate freely when the loading is light, but as it increases the ratchet comes into operation. When the sheet is eased, the load on the block is reduced, which releases the sheet.

Sheet Winches

On larger sailing craft, foresails can only be pulled in or sheeted by hand in light winds. In stronger winds, winches must be employed. These comprise a drum and a ratchet to limit movement. The difference between the basic sail winch and the snubbing winch is that on the former a handle can be used to rotate the drum, thus providing leverage.

Conventionally, the drum rotates only in a clockwise direction and therefore the sheet must be wound around the drum for adequate friction in this direction, whichever tack the boat is on. This can be

Fig 115   The mode of operation of this rope stopper is shown.

Fig 116   Bank of rope stoppers.

Winches are used extensively on sailing yachts, for example for halyards and many control lines. Not only does a winch enable a rope to be pulled with a greater force than could be applied directly, but increased control is permitted so that minute adjustments can be made.

A winch is an effective mechanism when there is little friction in its working parts and the effort expended is put to good use. Gearing reduces the efficiency slightly, but enables a greater load to be applied in pulling in a sail or making adjustments. The drawback is that there is more winding to do.

Rope Stoppers
(Figs 115 & 116)

Frequently, winches serve multiple purposes and, because the winch must be free of one rope before it can accommodate another, the rope must be cleated or retained at a point before the winch. *Rope stoppers* provide the most

effective means for achieving this. They are much more effective for the purpose than a cleat, can be released when under load and the rope can be winched in whilst the stopper is in the 'on' position. Rope stoppers are particularly useful for halyards.

Levers
(Figs 117 & 118)

Levers are efficient too. The over-centre catch principle is employed with some levers – used, for example, to tension the rigging or foresail halyard on a dinghy. Although the pick-up point on this kind of lever is usually adjustable, by its nature

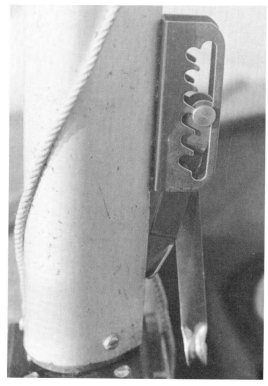

Fig 117   Tensioning lever, with adjustment, for the foresail halyard on a dinghy.

Fig 118   Kicking-strap lever. The wires attach to the boom and the base of the mast.

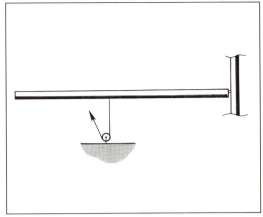

Fig 119   A mainsheet system with a velocity ratio of one to one.

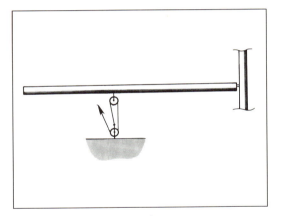

Fig 120   A velocity ratio of two to one.

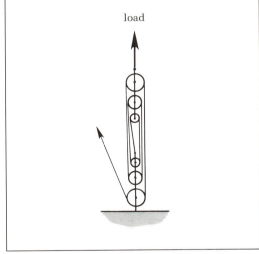

load

Fig 121   A tackle with a velocity ratio of six to one. The sheaves are normally mounted alongside each other rather than in line.

the lever must be either off or on. This can be useful as a means of achieving the level of tension desired in a foresail halyard or for permitting the shrouds to be slackened for downwind sailing and tensioned for sailing upwind.

Another popular type of lever is that used as part of a kicking strap. The role of the kicking strap is to prevent the boom rising and the mainsail twisting excessively and also, as far as dinghies

are concerned, to influence mast bend. A tackle may be attached to reduce further the amount of effort required to produce a particular amount of tension. Although convenient as a system for tensioning standing backstays on small cruisers, a drawback in the use of a lever for this application is that it may lack an adequate range of movement, with the consequence that the user may not be able to tension the backstay sufficiently.

This is one of the deficiencies of levers. The other is that of length. There may not be adequate space to house a lever if it is to provide sufficient leverage. These two deficiencies are inter-connected. The power of the lever can be increased by increasing the length of the effort part of the lever or by reducing the length of the part that provides tension, but the latter reduces the range of movement.

Screws

Screw-type systems, for example bottlescrews, enable much power to be applied in that the turning effort is small for the tension provided. The drawback is that the number of turns and the time taken are high in order to effect a relatively small change in distance. This is not a particular disadvantage for bottle-screws used to tension the standing rigging, but would be in the case of a backstay requiring fairly urgent, rapid adjustment.

One significant disadvantage of the bottlescrew is that friction is fairly high, although this is of benefit in preventing the bottlescrews from unwinding automatically. Releasing them requires effort and time, unlike most systems that free of their own accord.

Tackle
(Figs 119–122)

Mainsheet systems need to free immediately when released and, very commonly, tackles are employed. The

Fig 122   High friction limits the number of parts that can be used effectively.

mainsheet leads from the hand to a block, which should be attached to the boat and not the boom for a consistent *lead* and easy cleating.

If the mainsheet were to run simply from the block to the boom, it would have one *part* only, and a *velocity ratio* of one to one, implying that the speed at which the mainsheet can be hauled in is equal to the speed at which the boom is adjusted. If the mainsheet were to pass through a block on the boom and return to a fixing on the first block, it would have two parts and the velocity ratio would be two to one.

Mainsheets having a velocity ratio of two to one are used for small dinghies where the mainsail loadings are relatively low. For larger boats, a velocity ratio of six to one might be used and this system would comprise six parts.

If there were no friction in the system, the effort required for a velocity ratio of six to one would be one sixth of the load applied to the boom. Blocks for which the sheaves are of large diameter or of ball-bearing type present a low level of friction, particularly if the mainsheet is of small diameter. If there is a high level of friction in the system, the effort required might be as high as one quarter of the load for this six-part system.

For a high-friction system, the effort required is little reduced even when the number of parts is increased. There is a law of diminishing returns – increasing the number of parts from, say, ten to twenty would reduce the effort required only minutely but would still require twice as much rope to be hauled for the same boom movement.

If loads are high, so that many parts are called for, the efficiency of the system needs to be at a high level. So-called *muscle boxes*, used for mast rams and other adjustments on dinghies, use no more than about twelve parts because the gain is insufficient to warrant the use of further parts.

This highlights the main disadvantage with the simple tackle: friction limits the number of useful parts. The load hauled cannot be greater than ten or fifteen times the effort that can be applied, and even then there is much rope to haul through the system for a reasonable range of movement.

Cascade Systems
(Fig 123)

Yet, in the days before winches, sailing ships were managed using tackles with

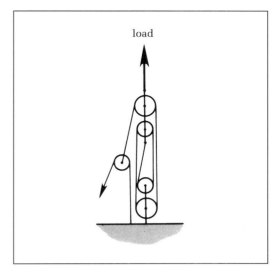

Fig 123   A cascade system. An additional block doubles the velocity ratio to ten to one. A turning block could be added if a different direction of lead is needed.

blocks of lower efficiency than are available today. The solution lay in multiplying the velocity ratio by using a tackle on the part normally hauled to produce what today is called a *cascade system*.

A simple two-part tackle interposed in this manner doubles the velocity ratio. For example, a two-part system added to a five-part results in a velocity ratio of ten to one. Because, in this example, only one additional block is employed, the loss due to friction is minimal and so the effort is nearly halved.

Mainsheet Fine Tune

A similar approach is adopted so that mainsheet systems have a *fine tune* capability, which utilizes a high velocity ratio for ease of handling. This is added to one end of the mainsheet system, the other end providing the normal, relatively coarse adjustment. The advantage of this system is that the boom can be hauled in quickly with the coarse adjustment, albeit with more effort, leaving the fine tune for the small adjustments that can be made with ease.

Spinnaker Hoisting
(Figs 124 & 125)

An extreme example of coarse adjustment in which a tackle is used in reverse is a feature of some dinghy spinnaker-hoisting systems. The length of rope hauled is half that of the hoist. Effectively, the effort is applied to the tackle rather than to the part. This does require more effort, but the objective is to raise the spinnaker quickly before it fills with wind.

Drum and Axle
(Figs 126)

Another system, although now fallen out of favour, is the *drum and axle* for which a relatively small effort manufactures a high load, such as for tensioning a kicking

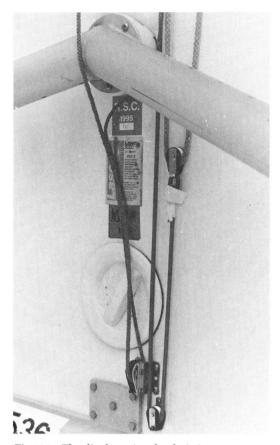

Fig 125   The dinghy spinnaker-hoisting system in practice.

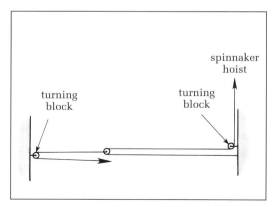

Fig 124   A schematic of a dinghy spinnaker-hoisting system.

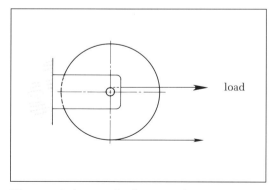

Fig 126   A drum and axle system for mechanical advantage.

strap. The principle is the same as for the lever or the winch with its handle: the effort is applied to a large drum that rotates an axle to which it is attached.

The plus point about the drum and axle is that the range of movement is not restricted as for the lever. The negative aspect is, as with the lever, one of space: in order for the drum and axle to provide a substantial advantage, the drum must be large, which may be difficult to accommodate at the base of a dinghy mast, for example. Another drawback of the drum and axle is that the wire used on the axle tends to bunch up and become damaged, producing broken strands to snag sails and fingers.

Systems Control

A dinghy kicking strap needs to be powerful so that the mainsheet can be arranged to pull in the mainsail without having to do duty as a kicking strap. The use of a *mainsheet hoop* or similar device raises the point at which the boom is sheeted so that this is achieved. It means that the dinghy helmsman can sheet the sail more easily and more precisely.

The system is not suitable where the boom needs to be sheeted up to or to windward of the centre-line. In this case a pair of *strops* provides a simple, lightweight solution. The strops lead to each side of the dinghy, the mainsheet block being attached at the joining point.

This allows the windward strop to be tensioned whilst the leeward one is slackened, enabling the block and thus the boom to be pulled to *weather*. It can be arranged so that, when the windward strop is tightened, the leeward one is released automatically. When tacking, the other strop is tightened, again releasing the new leeward strop. The worst thing about this system is that at times one or other strop is slack and when *gybing* both are slack, which provides the potential for tangles.

Mainsheet Tracks

Some dinghies and most yachts incorporate a *mainsheet track* positioned in the cockpit and running athwartships. The track carries a *mainsheet traveller*, to which the mainsheet block is attached. Yachts, which are closer-winded than dinghies, have a greater need for pulling the boom close to the centre-line and this requires that the traveller is pulled up to weather. Again, systems whereby one control line for the mainsheet traveller is released when the other is tensioned are feasible.

Very commonly, the traveller is shifted to leeward when reaching in order that the boom can be held down, supplementing the kicking strap. The mainsail position can then be adjusted by control lines to the traveller.

This system does restrict the capability to move the mainsail in and out quickly and powerfully via the mainsheet to respond to wind variation. From this point of view, the traveller should be placed on or above the centre-line even when sailing on a reach, and it could be argued that the kicking strap should be powerful enough to downhaul the boom by itself.

Another school of thought suggests that, with the traveller to leeward and the kicking strap under light tension, easing of the mainsheet in the gusts produces both twist and freeing of the mainsail. Twist permits air to be spilled effectively from the mainsail. But, for those who like better control, the crew can make adjustments to both mainsheet and kicking strap in order to meet both criteria.

Foresail Sheet Tracks
(Figs 127 & 128)

Tracks are frequently utilized so that changes can be made to the sheeting position of the foresails. The track may be sufficiently long to accommodate different sized foresails in the case of a yacht for which the wardrobe ranges from genoa to storm jib. The traveller permits easy adjustment of the fore-and-aft sheeting position. Unless clew height is raised, the shorter the foot, the further forward the sheeting position needs to be.

Adjustment of the traveller is also required for different wind strengths and for changes to the mast rake that place the clew in different positions. Although travellers located by a plunger in a hole in the track are straightforward, they do lack fineness of adjustment and, worse, cannot be adjusted under load. Since the traveller tends to be drawn aft by the direction of the sheet, control lines that pull the traveller forward are advisable,

Fig 128   The wide beam on this racing yacht exaggerates the narrow sheeting angle.

but provision must also be made to pull or hold it aft, otherwise it tends to be pulled forward when tacking and remain in that position.

Fore-and-aft foresail tracks are located in the hope that their distance from the centre-line is correct. This distance affects the *sheeting angle*, which should be as little as eight to ten degrees for a yacht sailing upwind, but adjustment is required in different wind strengths and sea conditions.

Barber Hauler

The solution would seem to be a track that can be moved or mounted transversely, but an easier solution is the

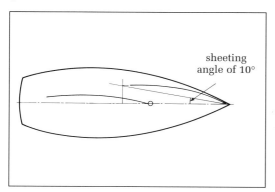

sheeting angle of 10°

Fig 127   The measurement of the foresail sheeting angle.

Fig 129   Mainsail outhaul turning block.

Fig 130   Multiple turning blocks on a large yacht.

Fig 131   Sheet lead with three rollers.

barber hauler, which is used to pull the sheet outboard. When operated in conjunction with the traveller, a wide range of sheeting positions is possible.

Improved efficiency in the rig when reaching comes about by sheeting as far outboard as possible. Without the barber hauler, the foresail becomes excessively full when the sheet is eased and the aft part of the sail curves inboard. The barber hauler has a part to play when sailing upwind too, particularly in fresh winds, as additional control can be achieved. In the gusts, the barber hauler line can be winched in, which pulls the sheet outboard and tensions it, achieving a desirably wider sheeting angle and a flatter sail.

Turning Blocks
(Figs 129–132)

Direction changes for the various sheets, halyards and other items of running rigging on yachts and dinghies are dealt with by using blocks that must be able to rotate freely in order to take up an angle so that binding does not occur.

Fixed blocks, such as those for the foresail sheets or the halyard exits are more problematical as they are fastened to the deck and mast respectively. Care must be taken at the design stage to ensure that the leads are true and friction is minimized.

Fig 132   Little change in direction for the rope means that sheaves can be omitted without a great increase in friction.

The sheaves of blocks must be of sufficient diameter that minimal practicable friction exists, but also so that rope is not damaged. This is particularly true for wire rope, used extensively for halyards because of its supreme low-stretch capability, for which a sheave diameter much less than twenty times the wire's diameter causes excessive deformation of the lay (the term given to the twisting of the strands).

Rope Damage

Deterioration of halyards results because the halyard is always loaded in the same place at the sheave when the sail is hoisted. Although aramid fibre rope is often used for halyards because of its especially low-stretch capability, like wire it does not take kindly to making abrupt turns.

Although pre-stretched Terylene will survive such abuse, it stretches too much, despite its description, to be practical. Perhaps the best solution for now is high modulus polyethylene rope, which offers low stretch, high resistance to damage and also low weight, though its high cost counts against it. Nevertheless, the cost of wire to which a rope tail must be spliced so that it can withstand winching is expensive enough.

Summary

- In order to alter mast bend and maintain high forestay tension on yachts, the backstay requires adjustment when sailing. Tackles of some form can be employed on yachts having fractional rigs and on masthead-rigged yachts of small size.

- Various other systems of mechanical advantage used on boats include winches, levers, screws, and drum and axle mechanisms.

- Tackles have wide application, but the load hauled relative to the effort applied is limited because of friction in the system, regardless of the velocity ratio employed. Cascade systems overcome this disadvantage.

- Convenient adjustment of the positioning of turning blocks used for the sheeting of sails improves efficiency. Turning blocks must align or be aligned with the lead.

7
MAKING THE BEST
OF THE RIG

The Nature of Sailing Balance

Generally, the designer, sail-maker, mast manufacturer and rigging specialist determine many of the characteristics of a sailing boat. Since each of these individuals or teams makes decisions based upon judgement, and compromises abound, it is for the sailor to adapt the boat to make the best of it, particularly if he or she wishes to compete.

Designer Balance

One important decision the designer makes is the positioning of the sail plan relative to the hull. Consideration is given to *balance* so that the boat does not require large amounts of *helm*, in which the rudder must be held at a large angle to maintain a course. For the cruising sailor, extremes of helm are tiring and for the competitor, slowing.

At the design stage, the designer will attempt to position the sail plan fore and aft so that it relates to the underwater profile, in particular the keel foil or centreboard – which limits side slip, known as *leeway*. If the sail plan is too far forward, the boat will tend to turn away

from the wind when sailing upwind. Conversely, if the sail plan is too far aft, the tendency will be for the boat to turn into or towards the wind.

Desirable Helm
(Fig 133)

Both tendencies need rudder to correct, the former requiring *lee helm* and the latter *weather helm*, which signify the directions in which one moves the tiller to maintain course. Although it might be supposed that zero helm is the most desirable, the rudder having least drag in this position, slight weather helm when sailing upwind is, in fact, preferable. Thus we have a desire for the boat to luff.

For the cruising sailor, weather helm provides 'feel' and is safer because the

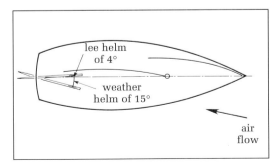

Fig 133   Weather and lee helm.

boat will turn into the wind if the helm is released. For the competitor, weather helm when sailing upwind assists progress because the rudder in this position pushes the boat into the wind. Greatest efficiency appears to be when between 3° and 5° of weather helm are required for sailing upwind. If the tiller (and hence rudder) are angled more than this, the resulting drag outweighs the push to windward.

Changing Balance

Although the positioning of the sail plan is determined by the designer, the amount of helm required can be adapted by those sailing the boat. Little can be achieved by re-positioning the mast within the limits normally available or by raking the mast.

Experiments indicate that the whole rig would need to be moved approximately 200mm (8in) to produce a 1° change in rudder angle for a 6m (20ft) boat, and this degree of shift would not normally be feasible. Similarly, the expectation that raking the mast will transform the balance is likely to be optimistic: 200mm (8in) of rake (or additional rake) measured at the top of the mast would produce perhaps one third of a degree of helm difference on a boat of this size.

The effect that rake may have is likely to relate more to the way the sails are working and the way the boat is sailed. Sailing people disagree hotly about how much rake should be used.

Effects of Heel

The factor that is more significant in affecting balance than rig positioning is the angle of heel. As the boat heels, the component of force that drives the boat forward moves further away from the boat's centre-line, producing a significant turning effect, which requires weather helm to keep the boat on course. Additionally, as the boat heels, the hull form presented to the water becomes asymmetrical, which contributes to the weather helm required.

This effect can be recognized in strong winds by the large amounts of weather helm needed by yachts when sailing upwind. The solution is to ensure that heel is not excessive, and this may warrant a change to a smaller foresail and perhaps reefing the mainsail. For racing, the crew, and movable ballast if allowed, also need to be positioned as far to weather as is feasible in order to minimize the heel.

When sailing upwind in light winds, yachts often carry lee helm, which has a greater slowing effect than weather helm because the side force produced by the rudder is pushing the boat away from the wind and it makes the hull and keel foil less efficient. The solution is to induce heel by moving the crew's weight to leeward.

Best Helm Angle

The same principle applies to dinghies, which can of course be heeled more readily. Again, in strong winds, excessive weather helm can be corrected by reducing heel. In general, dinghies are fastest when sailed fairly upright, which involves moving the crew outboard and spilling wind from the sails if necessary. It probably makes sense to think in terms of achieving the optimum helm angle rather than the principle of keeping the dinghy upright regardless.

Basically, the same technique can be used for minimizing the amount of helm required when sailing downwind. In this case, the rudder needs to be on the centre-line for best efficiency. If weather helm results, the dinghy or yacht should be heeled to weather as far as possible or as necessary to correct this wholly or in part. Lee helm would be corrected by heeling to leeward.

Assessing Rudder Angle

In reality, determining the amount of helm a boat is carrying is not easy because of the frequent adjustments that are made to the helm. It is probable that the tiller is usually played too much, with the attendant tendency to over-correct. One objective when sailing upwind in particular is to strike a balance between the need to achieve the boat's best angle to the wind and waves and the frequent tiller movement required for correction. The best angle may be outweighed by the slowing effect of tiller waggling.

Even in steady state conditions, the tiller angle may be difficult to determine. Appropriate marks can be made on the deck and the tiller extension so that measurements can be taken.

Balancing the Rudder

If the rudder and tiller assembly is not in balance, the helmsman can be mistaken in thinking that the dinghy (in particular) or small yacht has weather or lee helm in light winds when in fact it has not. When at rest, it should be possible to heel the boat by moving the crew to one side and for the tiller (and rudder) to remain on the centre-line.

Usually, the weight of the tiller and

buoyancy of the rudder causes the tiller to fall to leeward and this effect gives the impression of weather helm when sailing in light winds. Of course, if the rudder is heavy, the helmsman will be convinced, when sailing in these conditions with the boat heeled to encourage the sails to set, that the boat has lee helm.

Imbalance is overcome by subtracting or adding weight to the tiller or rudder as needed until balance is achieved when afloat. This helps the helmsman to sail with minimal use of the rudder.

Sail Shape

Sail shape affects balance too. If the position of the maximum draft drifts aft, then the force produced by the sail will do so as well, which will increase or create weather helm. Nevertheless, the change to the helm required would not be large.

It would be unwise to adjust the set of the sails so that the point of maximum camber is moved forward or aft in the hope of achieving improved sailing

Fig 134   Genoa with a camber of 19 per cent.

Fig 135 This mainsail has excessive camber of 18 per cent. The sail is backwinded noticeably by the genoa.

balance. The sails should be set for optimum efficiency in their own right.

Sail Shape Targets

The sails must be built and then set so that they adopt a shape that will be the most effective in driving the boat. To some extent this rests upon scientific principle and to some extent upon on-the-water experience. Room for experiment and opinion still remains.

Camber
(Figs 134–136)

Whilst camber can be expressed as the ratio of the draft and the distance between luff and leech (or *chord length*) at a particular height, it is more convenient to describe it in the form of a percentage.

The range between 12 per cent and 20

per cent covers the requirement for fore and aft sails (spinnakers being more effective if they are rather fuller). More precisely, for good performance upwind, it is thought that the foresail should have a camber of 14 to 16 per cent in very light, ghosting conditions; 18 to 20 per cent in light to moderate conditions; become progressively flatter with increasing wind speed to about 14 to 16 per cent in moderate to fresh conditions; and down to about 11 to 12 per cent in fresh winds.

Generally, the amount of camber required in the mainsail should be less than for the foresail, due to the backwinding effect of the foresail. A mainsail camber of 16 per cent or so in light winds through to 13 per cent in moderate winds and 10 per cent in fresh winds is in accord with the figures for the foresail.

It is usually held that camber should

Fig 136 With a high level of mast bend, the camber is 10 per cent as shown by the upper draft stripe and 14 per cent at the lower stripe.

not be uniform at all heights in a sail. The argument is that both mainsail and foresail should be flatter towards the foot and a couple of per cent fuller towards the top than in the middle.

It is supposed that the flatter foot reduces the vortex created in this region by air moving from the higher-pressure windward side to the lower-pressure leeward side, and that the fuller head makes this narrow part of the sail more effective.

Draft Position

The point of maximum draft would be slightly further aft at the head than at the foot. Foresails appear to be most effective with the maximum draft located about 42 per cent aft. In stronger winds and rough seas, a position slightly further forward lends more tolerance to the sail. Pointing capability is reduced but this is not a

Fig 137   Sail twist.

primary concern in these conditions; indeed, maintaining good boat speed takes priority.

In conditions in which the water is smoother and therefore the *apparent wind* more consistent, the foresail entry can be flatter for better pointing capability. Similarly, because of the backwinding effect of the foresail, the mainsail entry needs to be reasonably flat and the maximum draft at a position about 48 per cent aft.

Sail Twist
(Fig 137)

An element of *twist* needs to be given to both sails so that they fall away to leeward progressively towards the head. This accommodates the *angle of attack* of the wind, which meets the sails and the boat at a wider angle aloft than at deck level. The difference can be several degrees.

This phenomenon results from friction between the air and the water, which leads to lower wind speed at the deck than at the top of the mast. The result, as the boat sails upwind, is an apparent wind angle that is closer to the *true wind* angle aloft than at deck level – and hence the twist.

Adapting the Sail Shape

Adjustments to the rig to achieve the desired amount of camber, position of maximum draft and sail twist are inter-related. The starting point for users is with the sails already built by the sail-maker and the rigging layout utilized.

Although the amount of camber is determined in some measure by the cut of the sails, their setting has a significant influence. Mast bend reduces the mainsail camber as the luff curve is matched by the curve of the mast, as is shown in Figs 135 and 136. The sail-maker provides the user with this opportunity for varying mainsail camber.

Mast Bend for Yachts

In increasing wind, therefore, the mast is bent progressively. On a fractionally rigged yacht, this is achieved by tensioning the backstay, which pulls the top of the mast aft and thus pushes the middle forward. The running backstays principally increase forestay tension but the checkstays have a major influence on allowing or limiting bend.

If an aft-swept spreader rigging arrangement is used, the lowers should not be excessively tight or the mast bend achievable will be limited. For such rigs, it may be best to set up the rig with some initial bend in the mast, because the shrouds, and therefore lowers, must be tight in order to compensate for a lack of running backstays. It is not usual on a yacht of this kind that the shrouds would be adjustable to permit reasonable variation in mast bend.

Similarly, masthead-rigged boats may be limited in the degree of mast bend that can be achieved unless adjustable check stays and an inner forestay are fitted. Again, the mast can be set up initially with some bend to suit the mainsail, but this does mean that the adaptability of the rig is limited.

Mast Bend for Dinghies

Mast bend is readily enough achieved with the dinghy rig – which, because of its spreader arrangement, tends to be more flexible. The mast ram used at deck level on a keel-stepped mast provides good control of mast bend, as occurs on a yacht, and the kicking strap and mainsheet create bend in the mast, as does the backstay on a yacht.

The snag for the dinghy is that the tensioning of the kicking strap to produce mast bend also reduces the twist in the mainsail, which consequently may be less than is desirable. But the mainsail, mast and rigging work as a system when set up, usually designed to be able to adapt to differing conditions. Strong winds produce more twist in the mainsail, which can be controlled to an appropriate level by the kicking strap. This increases mast bend, thus flattening the mainsail, which essentially is required for strong winds.

Foresail Sheeting

Foresail twist is a function of sheeting position. Sheeting further aft increases twist because the leech is slackened relatively. The opposite occurs if the foresail is sheeted further forward.

A good starting point for establishing an initial sheeting position is by aligning the sheet with the middle point of the luff. It is to be noted that the sheet for a short-footed foresail will adopt a more vertical position than one for a large, overlapping foresail.

Leech and Luff Tension
(Fig 138)

Moving the foresail sheet lead forward has the effect of tensioning the leech and this shifts the position of maximum draft further aft. In a similar way, tensioning the luff moves the position of greatest draft further forward.

Luff tension provides the significant means whereby maximum draft can be positioned for the best efficiency, though the technique is somewhat limited for sails using structured materials. The halyards for both mainsail and foresail can be adjusted to vary luff tension, but if at their limit, and more luff tension is desired, the technique is to tension from the tack.

An eye, known as a *Cunningham hole*, is sewn into the sail above the tack and can be downhauled. This has much the same effect as tensioning the halyard. For a wire-luffed foresail, luff tension is adjusted by a Cunningham hole or by stretching the cloth over the wire.

The mainsail luff tension needs to be adjusted in line with mast bend. As the mast bends and sail camber reduces, the

Fig 138 Sliding luff on a jib that would be set flying, that is, not hanked to a stay.

point of maximum camber moves aft. Tensioning the luff restores the position of maximum camber.

Foot Tension

Tightening the foot of the foresail by sheet tension reduces camber in the sail. This results in an increase in the distance between luff and leech at any height – the sail is stretched out, having a camber-reducing effect on the whole of the sail.

Sheet tension tends to increase luff sag, which induces fullness and lessens the level of control that foresail sheeting has on camber. This emphasizes the importance of high tension in the forestay or wire luff.

The fullness of the mainsail can be modified in a similar way to the foresail but by using the mainsail clew outhaul. Hauling out the clew not only flattens the foot but has an effect on the whole sail. Mainsails that are loose-footed may be attached to the boom by a traveller at the clew, an arrangement that permits easy adjustment. More commonly, mainsails are fitted to the boom by a bolt rope and are therefore not so readily adjusted.

Flattening Reefs

So-called *flattening reefs* have some potential for reducing a yacht's mainsail camber in strong winds. An eye is formed in the mainsail leech some 300 to 400mm above the clew. In principle, this will flatten the sail if it is able to shorten the luff to leech distance.

Unless the leech is peculiarly angled as in the case of a low aspect ratio sail, there will be little gain if the sail cannot be pulled out beyond the clew position. Racing craft usually have a black band on the boom, signifying the limit to which the sail may be extended, and this may limit flattening if the foot is of full length.

More useful is the small reduction in area that the flattening reef confers, together with the rise in the boom at its aft end. Booms become lower with mast bend and the flattener compensates for this.

Sustaining Air Flow Over the Sails
(Figs 139 & 140)

Flattening the mainsail reduces its tendency to be backwinded by the foresail, particularly if it overlaps the mainsail by a large amount. Usually, the boom will need to be pulled towards or up to the centre-line of the boat. If the boom is pulled to weather of the centre-line, the force produced by the mainsail is likely to be in a sideways direction,

Fig 139   This mainsail is over-full and is backwinded despite the boom being nearly up to the centre-line.

producing heel rather than forward drive.

A better way of viewing the sheeting of the mainsail is in the context of the total sail plan. It helps to think of the mainsail and foresail as one unit, that is, as one aerofoil with a slot in it. For efficient windward performance, air from the leeward side of the foresail should pick up the air through the slot between foresail and mainsail and flow past the aft part of the mainsail.

Reading Flow
(Fig 141)

If the flow on the lee side of the mainsail breaks down, producing an eddy, or spasmodic flow reversal, efficiency is much reduced. Because the behaviour of the air is not visible, the technique of attaching so-called *tell-tales* in order to highlight flow is well established.

It has become the norm to stitch tell-tale strips of nylon cloth to points on the sails where flow is important or may be questionable (such as the leech of the mainsail). Good flow is demonstrated by the tell-tales streaming more or less in line with the sails. Poor or reversed flow results in one or more tell-tales collapsing

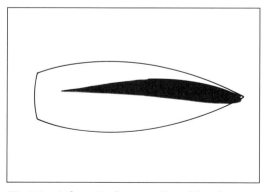

Fig 140   A theoretical perspective of the sloop rig as a single aerofoil.

Fig 141   A wind indicator helps to set the sails to advantage.

or pointing in a direction from leech to luff.

Mainsail Tell-Tales
(Fig 142)

The mainsail is sheeted accordingly in order to obtain satisfactory flow, though difficulty can arise in achieving flow at all heights. With fractional rigs in particular, the tendency is for the air to be bent from the foresail into the mainsail, whilst above the foresail the wind will be much more free, that is the angle of attack will be greater.

As a result, poor flow is likely to exist in the mainsail above the foresail. This can be corrected by setting the top part of the mainsail at a greater angle to the centre-line. The problem is exacerbated by the apparent wind effect, which results in the wind aloft being freer still.

The solution is to introduce twist in the sail (as in Fig 137) by easing the kicking strap and mainsheet and pulling the mainsheet traveller up to weather.

The various controls need to be manipulated until all leech tell-tales are streaming aft.

In smooth water, this condition is easy enough to identify. But in waves, the rig moves fore-and-aft significantly when sailing upwind as the boat pitches and this produces variations in the apparent wind. As a result, the tell-tales tend to alternate between streaming and collapsing and, when racing, the boat is sailed so that as much flow as possible is maintained. Cruising sailors are less fussy.

Foresail Tell-Tales
(Figs 143–144)

Tell-tales are placed towards the luff of foresails so that flow into the leading edge of the sail can be monitored. In fact, flow

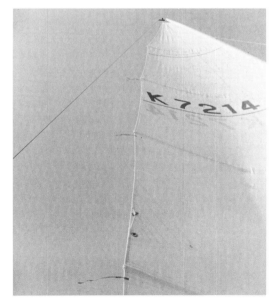

Fig 142   Air flow appears inconsistent at the top of the sail. The tell-tale just below the top batten has moved to the leeward side of the sail, due to the eddy in this region.

in this region is the most important of the whole sail plan, and the objective is to use the tell-tales to ensure flow is maintained over the leeward side of the foresail. Luff groove devices aid flow but can be less convenient than foresail hanks.

Several pairs of tell-tales are usually placed at points up the foresail. At each point, a tell-tale is attached on each side. The helmsman can normally observe the leeward tell-tale, which is the more important of the two, through the sail, though if the sun shines from the wrong direction this is not feasible. Better is to place the tell-tales, or at least one pair, in a small window.

Interpretation
(Figs 145–147)

If the leeward tell-tale does not stream aft but falls, probably accompanied by the windward tell-tale, this indicates that flow is unsatisfactory and either the boat needs to be steered more towards the wind or the foresail sheet needs to be eased.

When sailing upwind in light and variable winds, changing heading towards the wind takes longer than easing the sheet to re-establish flow, and so best practice is to get the leeward tell-tale streaming by letting out the sheet slightly and then pulling in as the helmsman brings the boat onto its best course relative to the wind.

The behaviour of the windward tell-tale provides further information on the setting of the foresail. When the tell-tale lifts, it signifies that the boat is being sailed as close to the wind as it reasonably can be, and the driving force relative to the heeling force is about as

Fig 143 Luff groove device that bears a similarity to the mast luff groove for the mainsail.

Fig 144 Jib hanks disturb the airflow in the foresail luff region but retain the sail when lowered.

Fig 145   Air flow has broken down on the leeward side of the foresail.

high as possible. This assumes that the leeward tell-tale is streaming.

Sail away from the wind just a few degrees and the windward tell-tale will start to stream also. At this angle to the wind, more driving force is being produced but at the expense of more heeling force.

In some sailing conditions, such as when a sea is running, the extra drive from sailing slightly free is beneficial. But in stronger winds, when heeling needs to be minimized, an angle to the wind in which the windward tell-tale is lifting is the more efficient.

The foresail tell-tales also give a pointer to whether the sail has an appropriate amount of twist. Sail towards the wind and the tell-tales should respond in unison. In the same way, if the top tell-tales tend to collapse when the lower ones show ideal flow, the indication is that there is too little twist in the sail.

Spinnaker Setting

In many respects, the spinnaker can be set using the same principles that apply to foresails. The asymmetric spinnaker, used by boats able to draw the apparent wind far enough ahead such that it is

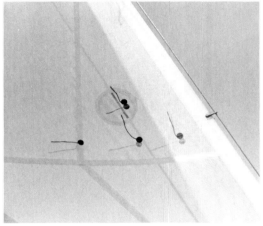

Fig 146   Sailing close to the wind. The driving force is high relative to the heeling force. Good for fresh winds.

Fig 147   Maximum drive but with an increase in heeling force. Good up to moderate winds.

feasible that the sail is tacked on the centre-line, are reminiscent of overgrown, full and lightweight genoas. The cruising 'chute and other variants favoured by cruising sailors display characteristics not dissimilar from those of the foresail.

Layout
(Figs 148 & 149)

The conventional spinnaker, which is symmetrical about a vertical centre-line, is tacked to a spinnaker pole that attaches to the mast at a variable height on the windward side of the boat. It is then sheeted to leeward. The spinnaker tack and pole are restrained by the guy.

The system presents a number of variables that provide adjustments to camber, position of maximum draft and twist just as occurs with a foresail, though the built shape of the spinnaker is more dominant.

Reaching

A general principle applying to the setting of the spinnaker is that the pole

Fig 149   When set, the spinnaker spreads. Keeping it on the point of collapse ensures that flow is maintained over the leeward side of the sail.

Fig 148   With all three corners stretched out, the 'built' shape of this spinnaker can be seen.

should be positioned perpendicularly to the wind, and the sail sheeted so that the luff is on the point of collapse. This configuration proves satisfactory on a broad reach when the wind is abaft the beam. When the wind is on the beam, the pole can be pulled round so that it is closer than perpendicular to the wind. The greater the distance the spinnaker pole is from the forestay, the more forward is the force from the spinnaker.

When the pole is against the forestay, the wind forward of the beam and the spinnaker sheeted hard in order to set it, the decision arises as to whether the genoa could be more productive at this angle to the wind. Certainly, the spinnaker produces significantly more heeling force. In fresh winds, pulling the spinnaker pole away from the forestay reduces a yacht's heel and the chances of rounding into the wind uncontrollably, termed *broaching*.

Just as tensioning the luff of a foresail moves the maximum draft forward, so lowering the pole has a similar effect. Shifting the fullness of the spinnaker forward slightly on a reach is of benefit to the performance of the sail.

Further Shaping

The sheeting position also affects the shape of the spinnaker. If sheeted too far forward, more camber is induced and the leech turns the air towards the mainsail. This is not an efficient shape, tending to produce drag and heeling force.

Reaching in moderate to fresh winds requires that the pole is reasonably high and the spinnaker sheeted well aft in order that its shoulders will spread. Lighter winds require a different spinnaker set for best performance and both clews can be lowered slightly by sheeting further forward and dropping the pole.

Although the generally held guide that the clews should remain level is fairly sound, it is better to vary the sheeting position and the pole height according to the overall shape of the spinnaker.

Level Pole?

Another commonly held view is that the pole should be level or parallel to the deck in order to project the tack of the spinnaker as far as possible. Whilst true geometrically, it may not be profitable to shift the pole to make it level if the business of racing the boat is upset.

If a 2m (6ft) pole were 5° out of level, the loss of projection is only 8mm (0.3in). At 10°, the loss becomes more significant at 30mm (1.2in), although it could hardly be regarded as avoidable at all costs.

Sailing Downwind
(Fig 150)

When sailing downwind, the pole should be slightly forward of a position square to the wind, or the force from the spinnaker will be excessively towards the windward side of the boat.

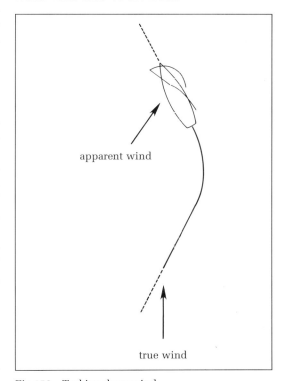

apparent wind

true wind

Fig 150   Tacking downwind.

In light winds, the sail needs to be reasonably full and therefore the pole should be fairly low and the spinnaker sheeted forward of its normal position. In moderate breezes, the aim is to spread the sail in order to produce a large projected area, so the pole should be reasonably high and the sheet should pull out the clew rather than pull it down.

However, in strong winds there is some benefit, in the case of yachts, in lowering the pole and sheeting from a forward position in order both to stabilize the spinnaker and reduce the projected area by closing in the shoulders to a degree. This also helps if or when the yacht rolls. Shifting the pole forward somewhat and sheeting the sail to a greater degree than usual minimizes the rolling tendency.

Tacking Downwind
(Fig 150)

Better still is to sail not directly downwind but at an angle to the wind, though this may require gybing to reach the objective. This may be a faster way to sail, though is less likely to be so in strong winds in the case of yachts.

For boats that are able to reach high speeds, sailing at an angle to the wind results in increased apparent wind, leading to an improvement in speed that more than offsets the extra distance sailed. When sailing directly downwind, the speed of the boat inevitably is less than the wind speed.

The technique described as *tacking downwind* is used to good effect by multihulls and faster dinghies in all winds, and by yachts and slower craft in all but strong winds when a reasonable increase in boat speed results from the increase in the apparent wind (*see* Fig 150). It is seen that high-speed craft can use asymmetric spinnakers tacked on the centre-line although this means of setting would not be so efficient for slower craft.

Playing a Tune on the Rigging
(Fig 151)

In conjunction with 'tuning' the sails, the rigging can also be 'tuned'. Indeed, the common use of the term, analogous with piano tuning, appears more appropriate when applied to the rigging. The tension of the rigging is of great importance because of the way it supports the mast and affects its bending characteristics.

Setting up the mast and rigging for a dinghy is simpler than for a yacht. Multiple-spreader rigs, or even single-spreader yacht rigs and their adjustment, are complex.

Fig 151   A multiple-spreader rig, which would have required comprehensive setting up.

The basic steps in setting up a yacht's rigging involve first adjusting the mast rake fore and aft, then ensuring that the mast is upright and straight transversely by adjusting the rigging from the top downwards. Final adjustments are undertaken whilst sailing when the leeward bottlescrews can be tightened when under least load.

Initial Setting Up

By way of example, a single-spreader rig is considered. With the shrouds slack, the backstay and forestay are tensioned to give the desired aft rake, typically two to five degrees. The rake can be measured by hanging a weight on a halyard and measuring its distance from the mast at deck or coachroof level.

The next stage is to tension the cap shrouds (to a tension equal to one tenth of the boat's weight is often quoted). It is necessary to ensure that the mast is upright transversely, which is best assessed by measuring from the position of the cap shrouds to the chainplate on either side of the boat. This can be accomplished by hoisting a steel tape attached to the foresail halyard.

For the initial setting up, the lowers are tensioned to a level slightly below that of the cap shrouds, ensuring that the mast is straight laterally by sighting up the mast track. (Some fore-and-aft pre-bend might be present.)

On the Water

Final tensioning and adjustment are accomplished whilst sailing, ideally in a moderate breeze. In particular, the leeward shrouds are tensioned whilst sailing upwind, by two turns or so of the bottlescrews at a time. The yacht then is tacked so that the bottlescrews on the other side can be adjusted by the same increment in order to maintain the mast's verticality.

The shrouds are tightened until the leeward cap shroud is slack when sailing, but not loose. The lowers are adjusted so that the mast remains straight laterally on both tacks. This may place the lowers under more tension than the cap shrouds.

Fore-and-aft adjustments to the mast and rigging very much relate to the way they match the sails and wind conditions. Suffice it to say that mast bend flattens the mainsail and forestay tension improves the set of the foresail.

Summary

- Only minor adjustments to sailing balance can be made by adjustments to the rig. The effect of heel has a more prominent influence and this provides the racing crew with the means for sailing with the least use of the rudder.

- Camber in fore-and-aft sails should be between 12 and 20 per cent. An element of sail twist is needed. Tell-tales provide the means for ensuring that flow is maintained over the leeward side of the sail at all heights when sailing both upwind and at greater angles to the wind.

- The setting of the spinnaker can be likened to that of a genoa, but with more camber. The sheeting position and pole height affect camber.

- Setting up the rig of a yacht starts with adjusting the stays for desired mast rake. Then the shrouds are tightened, in order, from the top downwards. Final adjustments should be made by tensioning the leeward shrouds progressively whilst sailing.

8
CARE AND
MAINTENANCE

Taking Care of Sails

There are certain precautions that can be taken to prolong the life of sails and they mostly fall into the 'what not to do' category.

Fig 152 Sails are damaged more when allowed to flog than when set.

Flogging Sails
(Figs 152 & 153)

One of the primary causes of wear to fabric and stitching is flogging – allowing the sails to flap vigorously back and forth whilst on the mooring or dinghy hard. In the case of dinghies, it is best not to hoist the sails and then disappear to the race briefing. For sailing craft that are moored, raise the mainsail shortly before casting off and then the foresail when under way. When motoring in light winds, leave the mainsail folded on the boom.

Fig 153 Foresail furlers. Graduated padding is used in the luff of the foresail in order to assist the set.

Fig 154   The dark cloth indicates the protective fabric.

Many cruisers now have furling gear on the foresails, obviating the need to raise or lower them, thereby reducing the amount of folding and crazing of the fabric. Nevertheless, furled foresails create their own problems from exposure to sunlight.

UV Degradation
(Fig 154)

Probably the greatest cause of deterioration to sails is ultra-violet light, so *sacrificial strips* should be added to foresails that are left furled. A sacrificial strip is a piece of sail-cloth, usually of a dark colour, sewn onto the leech and foot of foresails so that, when correctly furled, the coloured strip protects the sail-cloth proper from ultra-violet light. The strip can be replaced when it disintegrates, without affecting the rest of the sail. Mainsails left on the boom can be protected by a sail cover when not in use.

Flaking Sails
(Figs 155–157)

Before fitting a mainsail cover, make sure that the outhaul is slackened. Ideally, the mainsail should be removed from the boom if it is not needed within the near

Fig 155   Large flakes should be used so that the folded sail does not fall to one side or other of the boom.

Fig 156   Flaking the foresail. The task is relatively easy in such calm conditions.

future, but it is unlikely that this is adhered to by any but the most angelic, so the usual action is to *flake* the mainsail over the boom, in 'concertina' folds. The flakes, or folds, should be perpendicular to the leech, which avoids the need to remove the battens. The folds need to be fairly large so that they droop over and hang down below the boom, ready for the sail cover to be fitted. It is advisable to secure the sail in some way, usually with sail ties comprising short lengths of tape, before fitting the cover.

The flaking of foresails is more difficult on board a yacht because of the lack of space. Genoas need to be flaked with the foot of the sail extending from the bow over the coachroof. One person at each end then takes bag-sized folds starting from the foot. Finally, the sail is

folded or rolled from clew and tack to fit the sail bag. Care must be taken when flaking sails that creases do not occur, particularly at the leech.

Wire-luffed foresails are better rolled than flaked. The resultant roll then is folded, ensuring that a fold does not run across the plastic window, if fitted.

Each of the luffs of large spinnakers can be flaked in order to ensure separateness so that twisting is less likely when hoisted. But the folding techniques used for fore-and-aft sails cannot be used for modern spinnakers. Fortunately, nylon spinnaker cloth is thin and resilient and can stand being stuffed into bags with little risk of damage.

Laminated Sails
(Figs 158–161)

By contrast, laminated sails need more careful handling. Although commonly flaked, the extreme bend in the fabric at the folds can be damaging, although this

Fig 157   Final folding or rolling to fit the sail bag. Care must be taken to ensure that the odd creases or folds in the leech are smoothed out as the sail is rolled.

is less true for the cruiser-type laminated sails, which are softer and more pliable.

For racing, it is common to have the foresails to be used flaked and ready so that they can be brought on deck and hoisted more quickly. For minimum fabric damage, and certainly for long-term storage, rolling is to be preferred.

In order to contain the flaked or rolled sail, a long zippered bag is used, sometimes called a *burst bag*, with double-ended nylon zips that pull apart easily. The resultant package is long and the urge to fold it is best resisted. Laminated sails also are vulnerable to abrasion. It is sensible not to drag such sails across tarmac, if cleaning or rolling

Fig 159   ... and flaked.

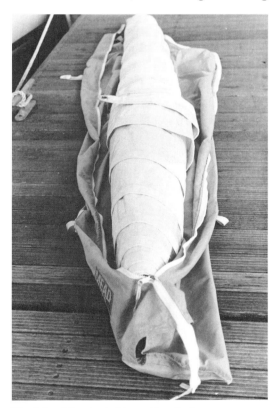

Fig 158   A laminated foresail, rolled ...

Fig 160   The laminated sail is contained by the burst bag.

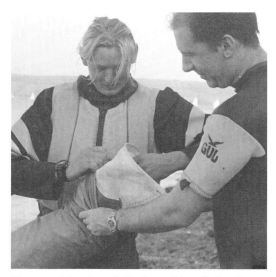

Fig 161   A laminated dinghy sail is rolled and pushed into its long bag.

ashore, as the polymer film can be damaged. If a single-sided laminate, the filaments might snag.

For small sails, as on sailboards, a length of plastic drainpipe can usefully be employed to roll the sail around, having first removed the battens. Some sailboarders roll their sails around the mast and use a fabric sleeve or drainpipe for transport.

Do-It-Yourself Cleaning

Most sail-makers offer a cleaning service for sails and often include storage in the charges, but it is possible to wash them yourself and remove the stains that sails seem to pick up during the season.

Smaller Sails

The least that ought be done is to hose them down to remove the salt deposits and this must be carried out before any other cleaning method is undertaken. Washing is best completed whilst the sails are suspended from a suitably strong line. Just peg out the sails by the luffs and spray them thoroughly with a reasonably strong jet of water on both sides, giving special attention to the seams where salt deposits can build up.

If the sails are small enough to fit in the bath without undue folding, and this would usually include spinnakers, then they can be immersed in water to which a small amount of soap flakes has been added, and agitated simply by pushing them under the water and allowing the soap to float off the grime. The water should not be hot or any resin coating could be damaged irreparably. Rinse thoroughly in several changes of water.

Acres of Canvas

With larger sails, there are two ways of tackling the washing process. One is to spread the sail on the ground, having first swept it meticulously to remove any potentially damaging stones and making sure that there are no oil or fuel deposits for the sail to soak up. Take a soft brush or broom and a bucket of soap flakes in solution and gently brush it onto the sail, taking care if you have to walk over it.

The second method, if the area is not large enough to spread the sail, is to peg it on a line, doubling the sail as necessary. Rinse the sail and then apply the soap solution with a cleaned spray bottle – such as is commonly available in supermarkets containing anything from window cleaning liquid to worktop foam. For a faster job, a purpose-made garden sprayer pressurized by a pump handle will make short work of it, but make sure that there are no chemical residues in the reservoir first. When the sail is saturated, give it a gentle scrub with the soft brush. (If the sail is doubled, some re-arranging will be required to cover all the surfaces.)

After either method has been employed, thoroughly rinse the sail with the hose, making sure you remove all traces of soap. The sail can then hang until it is dry, preferably out of direct sunlight, taking care that it is not dragging on the ground.

Stain Removal

Following washing and drying, the next thing is to tackle the stains. The approaches listed should cover the common eventualities applying to polyester and nylon but, if in doubt, a sail-maker will be able to advise on any stubborn or unusual stains.

All these treatments should be carried out on dry sails unless otherwise stated. Always try the relatively harmless remedies first, progressing to the chemical applications as a last resort. It is safest to wear plastic gloves and goggles when chemicals are used and to work in a well-ventilated area. If in doubt about the effect of the chemical on the sail-cloth, test on a spare piece first.

Blood This should be removed preferably when it is still fresh, by soaking in or applying cold water or, if this is not possible at the time, saliva. If the blood has had time to dry it will need a longer soak, followed by the application of a liquid detergent, still with cold water, until any residue has disappeared.

Oil and tar One of the simplest and most pleasant remedies is to apply eucalyptus oil and rub into the stain. Leave for an hour and wash off with a little washing-up liquid and water. This may require more than one application, but is less harmful to you and the environment than perchloroethylene, trichloroethylene or white spirit, all of which can be employed if absolutely necessary.

An alternative is a hand cleaner such as Swarfega (but not one that contains abrasive particles). This should be applied to the stain, left for 15 to 30 minutes and rinsed off with warm water.

Grease and wax Again, a hand cleaner can be used as above. Proprietary stain removers can also be employed, and these are available in small, colour-coded bottles from most supermarkets. They should be tested on some scrap sail-cloth first.

Mildew This is something that forms even on nylon and polyester as it is encouraged by grime and salt already present. Soak the affected part in a solution of one part bleach to ten parts cold water for about two hours. Rinse with plenty of cold water.

Paint and varnish There is absolutely no reason for paint and varnish to find their way onto sails any more than old engine oil or the dregs from the teapot would. The yearly re-varnishing of toe-rails and hatch covers should take place when all sails have been removed to the safety of their storage location, which should be well away from any paint or varnish cans, open or otherwise.

Rust Allowing sails to come into contact with stowed cans or tools will result in areas becoming stained with rust. Oxalic acid crystals, dissolved in warm water, can be sponged onto the stain, then rinsed off with fresh water. (Oxalic acid can be purchased from smaller chemists.)

Stains on Laminates

Film laminate sails are easier to clean, being smooth and non-porous, but are also easy to ruin with chemicals, so most dirt and stains should be tackled only with water, liquid detergent and non-scratch bathroom cleaning products.

Elements of Sail Repair

It is possible to do running repairs on sails, by hand or machine, and a prudent stitch or patch at the right time can save a huge repair later on. It is worth putting together a sail repair kit and keeping the smaller items in a purpose-made canvas ditty-bag or a large plastic container.

Sail Repair Kit

- Sail-maker's palm – for hand sewing

- Sail-maker's needles – for handwork

- Beeswax in a block – for waxing thread

- Scissors – pointed, for unpicking thread and cutting

- Knife – sharp, for general cutting

- Awl – for making holes

- Pliers – for gripping needles

- Hammer – for use with punches

- Hole punches – for making eyes

- Sail-maker's thread – for hand-sewing

- Whipping twine – for rope ends

- Sail-cloth offcuts – for patches

- Webbing – synthetic, about 12mm wide for reinforcement

- Sail repair tape – for temporary repairs

- Double-sided sticky tape – for assisting in holding repairs together

- Electrical tape – for taping jaws of pliers and general purposes

- Contact adhesive – for general gluing

- Proprietary hot-knife, a sharpened soldering iron, or a kitchen knife that can be heated – for cutting and heat-sealing sail-cloth

- Cigarette lighters – for sealing the ends of rope and thread

- Sewing machine – preferably heavy duty but domestic will suffice

- Sewing machine needles – sizes 14 and 16

- Silicone spray – for lubrication of sewing machine needles

- An assortment of hardware – hanks, slides, eyes, D-rings, round rings and turnovers

Hand Sewing
(Figs 162 & 163)

A *sail-maker's palm* is a leather strap that fits over the palm of the hand and incorporates a thumb hole and a metal cup with indentations to stop the eye end of the needle slipping as it is pushed through the work, rather in the way a sewing thimble works.

Using a palm is easily mastered, the action always being away from the body as the needle is pushed through. If the needle becomes hard to pull through, a

Fig 162   Tools useful for hand work.

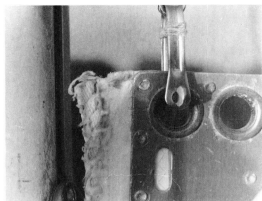

Fig 163   This luff is ready for some hand repair work.

pair of pliers can be used with electrical tape applied to the jaws so that the needle does not become roughened.

Use sail-maker's twine and draw it through the beeswax block a few times to lubricate it and prevent tangling during

Fig 164   Colour-matched patches will be used for this L-shaped tear.

sewing. Make the stitches even and taut, without puckering the fabric. Hand sewing is suitable for short lengths of seaming, small holes that can be darned and patches on parts of the sail that are inaccessible to a sewing machine. The method is also used where the thickness of the fabric would make it too hard for the machine needle to punch through, particularly if using a domestic machine.

Using a Sewing Machine
(Fig 164)

Most modern domestic machines can cope with spinnaker nylon and light-weight polyester. The most useful feature is zigzag stitch, as this is required for patches and batten pockets as well as seams.

It is important to test the stitching on some scrap sail-cloth of the same weight as the repair item and experiment with needle size and tensioning. The thicker the fabric, the larger the needle and the greater the tension required. If the stitches are too loose they will tend to chafe.

113

Patching Sails

Patching is a common sail repair, mostly for tears caused by sails catching on items of rigging that are not taped or protected in some way. Often quite jagged holes and rips are formed and the best way to deal with these is to apply a patch of similar sail-cloth to one side of the sail.

The patch should be cut to overlap the torn area by a small amount all round, and the edges should be heat sealed by cutting with a hot knife or equivalent. At this stage, the tear should not be trimmed or cut back for fear of disturbing the set of the fabric any more than necessary, particularly if the sail is old and will have stretched somewhat.

Ensuring that the warp and weft of the patch line up with those on the sail, the patch can be taped or glued in place ready for sewing. If using a machine, the sail may have to be folded or rolled in order for it to pass through the throat of the machine. Two rows of zigzag stitching around the edges should be sufficient on small patches. Finally, the torn parts of the sail beneath the patch can be trimmed with care using a hot knife.

Even very large tears should be repaired in the manner described. Replacing panels may seem appropriate, but it is unlikely that the original sail shape can be restored. The sail is more likely to retain its set by extensive local repair than by dabbling with significant replacement of sail-cloth.

Chafe Patches
(Fig 165)

The use of *chafe patches* falls into the category of 'preventive care' and entails applying patches to those areas that are likely to rub and wear, such as where genoas rub on the lifelines during downwind sailing or on the spreaders and shrouds. Use iron-on sail repair tape in a colour to match the sail and add a couple of rows of stitching around the edges.

Seams

Seams that have become unstitched or require adjustment can be sewn along the existing lines of stitching, applying an element of tension by stretching the seam as it is going through the throat of the machine. Double-sided tape can be used to stick the two panels together before sewing, though this can cause the machine to labour somewhat as the needle picks up the adhesive. A lubricant, such as a silicone spray, will limit clogging when applied to the needle.

Fig 165   Sensible shroud protectors on a cruiser minimize damage to the genoa.

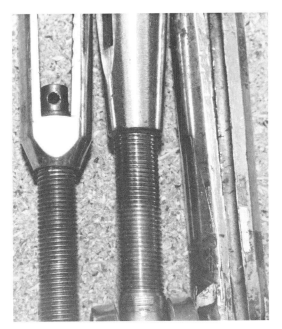

Fig 166   Bottlescrew damage. Thread damage and a crack in the corner of the opening in the bottle (left). Thread damage from screwing when under load and/or seized (centre). Damage to the bottle resulting from abuse (right).

Mast and Rigging Checks
(Fig 166)

The materials used for the modern mast and its associated fittings and rigging are corrosion-resistant and durable. Together with effective design and construction of the components, they reduce the need for frequent checks. The frequency of checking the rigging depends upon the extent of use and the consequences of failure.

Material Checks

One drawback in the use of the materials currently used, such as aluminium alloy and stainless steel, is a proneness to fatigue. Fatigue arises from use, in particular from large numbers of alternating stresses, which include light loadings, repeatedly applied and released.

For aluminium alloy and stainless steel, fatigue manifests itself in the form of cracks. An important check, best carried out when the mast is lowered so that close and careful inspection can be undertaken, is for cracks in the vicinity of welds and stress concentrations, such as occur around the holes in which halyard boxes are fitted.

Usually, cracks begin slowly. Forget about the crack-arresting technique of drilling a hole at the end of the crack so that the crack will not propagate. Replacement or professional repair is demanded.

Damage and Distortion

A typical end-of-season check would include the inspection of all components for evidence of damage or distortion. Clevis and shackle pins may be bent, resulting in uneven bearing stresses

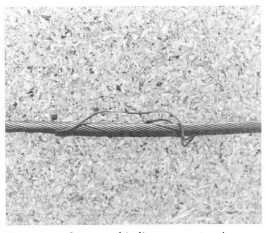

Fig 167   Broken strand indicates overstressing.

where the pin passes through the link; shroud T-terminals may have produced distortion in the plate attaching to the mast; there might be dents in the mast where it has been supported at the deck or coachroof.

Rigging Checks
(Fig 167)

Strands might have broken within the rigging wire. Free strands from 1 × 19 stainless steel standing rigging strongly invite replacement of the wire. The odd broken or free strand in 7 × 19 construction used for running rigging is less serious from a strength point of view, although handling becomes unpleasant.

It can be quite difficult to spot the odd loose strand, but a good starting point to look is where the wire makes severe turns, such as over halyard sheaves. The method not to be recommended is running your hand along the wire – the penetration of the wayward strand can be surprisingly painful.

Running rigging of fibre rope similarly suffers damage from making severe turns, but normally possesses greater resilience than wire. Where rope chafes, fibres become broken signifying remedial action. However, where a braided sheath is used, damage may occur to the sheath, resulting in only a small loss of strength whilst the core remains intact.

Any thinning of a fibre rope to wire splice indicates the need for further investigation.

Examining for Corrosion
(Fig 168)

Although not liable to corrosion, checks should be made to the mast and rigging

for advanced galvanic action arising from dissimilar metals in close proximity. Surface corrosion, such as where the anodizing or surface coating of the mast is damaged, is not serious. But in some areas, corrosion can advance quite rapidly.

The base of a keel-stepped mast is one such example. Salt water is liable to lodge in this area and the attachment of a cast alloy step fastened in place and sitting on a framework can result in rapid deterioration, probably of the mast itself.

Corrosion affects rigging wire, particularly where it terminates at fittings, and checks need to be made in these areas. Components comprising

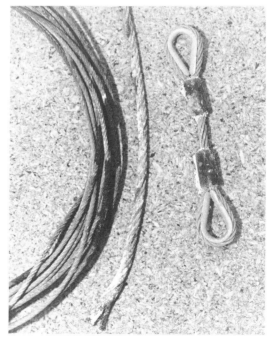

Fig 168 All three wires were left in close contact in a moist environment. The galvanized steel wires (left and centre) show corrosion and rust, and the copper ferrules on the stainless steel wire (right) have hastened corrosion due to galvanic action.

Fig 169   The ends of the spreaders need to be raised slightly

Fig 170   This spreader end is likely to damage the genoa.

mechanisms need not be especially liable to corrosion because they are usually treated with lubricants, which have a protective function.

'As-Built' Checks
(Figs 169 & 170)

The checking process should include the 'as-built' aspects of the rigging. A tour around a marina reveals a large number of yachts with spreaders that are at the wrong angle to the mast when the yacht is viewed either from the bow or stern. The spreaders should meet the shrouds so that there is no tendency for the outboard end of the spreader to be pushed up or down by the shroud.

Inadequate padding of the spreader ends may have been provided or there may be none at all. This can produce significant chafe on the genoa when tacking. Boots and wheels are available and can be fitted even where not supplied originally.

Occasionally, shroud attachments to the deck are incorrectly angled. Although toggles can accommodate the error, the clevis pin may have a poor bearing. Correction might be difficult. Before attempting judicious bending – which probably would require the removal of the piece of hardware – it might be best to seek advice, perhaps from the original supplier or manufacturer.

Effecting Maintenance and Repairs

It makes sense to hose or wash down the mast, rigging and fittings fairly regularly in the case of a dinghy, and at the end of the season for yachts that live on moorings. Salt is hygroscopic (it attracts moisture), which promotes the conditions required for corrosion.

A cleaning agent can be employed – which should not be a detergent because these products include constituents that themselves are corrosive. It is safer to use a hand soap, soap flakes or perhaps the soap pellets used with a pressure washer for cars.

The Mast

Water should be directed to the interior of the mast through a halyard box and allowed to drain out, if necessary by removing one of the boxes. Assuming that the mast has been lowered, it can be tilted so that water will run out of the bottom. There should be a drain hole at the lowest point so that water will drain readily from the mast when stepped. The drain hole may need probing at intervals to ensure that it is clear. Reasonably thorough treatment should be given to the inside of the mast. Although the anodizing process extends to the inside of the tube, it is less effective here and, short of the use of fibre optics, the interior cannot be inspected.

Painted masts are more vulnerable to corrosion because it is feasible to paint only the exterior. Hollow wooden masts can be varnished or coated on the inside before assembly, perhaps using epoxy or polyurethane finishes that are highly durable and, short of imperfections in the coating, offer a good level of protection.

Anodized aluminium alloy masts can be protected to some degree by a silicone-based wax polish. The mast can be waxed both at the end of the season with storage in mind and at the beginning to deal with the marine environment. Wax polishes possess different properties that are not revealed fully by advertising, but one that provides ultra-violet light protection is preferable. Anodizing is prone to fading, the darker colours being most affected. Black anodizing, in particular, fairly rapidly becomes grey in colour.

Lubricating

Lubricants containing silicones, Teflon or PTFE prove the most suitable for lubricating the moving parts of fittings. Before application, old lubricants can be removed with solvents such as white spirit. Generally, it is better not to use oils and greases, which attract dust and tend to dry out, becoming sticky. Also, some plastic materials are affected adversely by oil.

However, components like winches are lubricated specifically using oil and grease. Waterproof grease for the purpose is available. The working parts are not exposed and are subject to a high load that justifies the use of such lubricants.

Dismantling

Winch manufacturers specify a fairly exacting schedule for maintenance, which involves initial dismantling. For simpler components, such as a spinnaker halyard lead block, there is little value in disassembly, provided the parts rotate freely, there is no obvious wear and locking devices such as split pins are sound and not likely to catch sails, hands or whatever.

If a sheave does not rotate freely and does not free up fully and readily with lubrication, it is not good policy to continue lubricating in the hope that it will free. In cases like this, the best result is achieved by dismantling. It can happen that components do not work satisfactorily and no explanation can be found without dismantling. Dismantling uncovers all.

Repair Strategies
(Fig 171)

Frequently, logic enables simple fittings that do not function properly to be corrected. Often, repairs are possible. For example, a spinnaker sheet snap-shackle, specifically designed so that it frees readily, may not do so. If the body has distorted so that alignment is imperfect, replacement might be necessary, perhaps with a stronger snap-shackle. But, depending upon the circumstances, repair may well be feasible, for example by using a file to remove the material that is limiting movement.

Although such techniques are frowned upon by the professionals and those sailors who do not flinch at the price of a snap-shackle, there is a bonus in this repair-it-yourself approach: your understanding of the way the fittings work is enhanced, as is your ability to engineer solutions. This is a valuable skill for the long-distance sailor who may need to effect on-passage repairs.

Replacement Schedules

No matter how impecunious the owner, replacement at intervals of apparently sound components is often called for because of the potential effects of fatigue. An example is the standing rigging, which is earmarked for replacement every seven to ten years. (Two years or less might be a suitable replacement

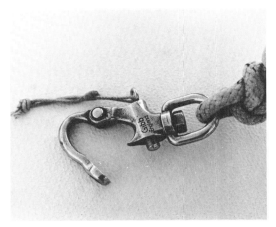

Fig 171 Snap shackle.

interval if the boat is subjected to extensive, arduous use.)

Such suggestions are based upon experience relating to the length of time standing rigging lasts in service, or indeed when it fails. Nevertheless, it takes a degree of courage to scrap a set of apparently sound standing rigging and replace it with an expensive, seemingly identical set.

The replacement interval mentioned would be typical of 1×19 stainless steel wire. The reduced flexibility of rod rigging and the extreme tendency of the material to fatigue indicate a similarly reduced working life. Two years is about it, which is unlikely to make the owners of yachts with rod rigging flinch because, if they cannot afford to replace it, they couldn't have afforded to buy it.

Running rigging is given a working life of about three to four years. Because the consequences of failure are less significant than for the standing rigging, this period could perhaps be extended. Applying a time limit of this order for wire running rigging seems reasonable, but, with careful inspection, fibre rope can be used for a very long time. Halyards and other ropes can be turned end-for-end so that the wear takes place at a different position.

Replacing Halyards

Internal halyards are most easily replaced if the existing halyards are still in place. The new halyard can be pulled through by attaching it to the old one, stitching them together for minimum bulk.

If it is necessary to re-reeve a new halyard, the first step is to pass a messenger (a thin cord) through the mast. With the mast upright, a short length of small link chain is attached to the messenger and fed through the appropriate halyard sheave. The messenger is hooked out at the exit point and then the halyard is pulled through by the messenger. In order to hook out the messenger or feed in the chain, it may be necessary to remove the sheave boxes temporarily.

When the mast is horizontal and cannot be raised to an upright position, some inventiveness is called for. It might be possible to attach the messenger to another halyard, or to use a length of wire that is fed through in order to lead the messenger.

Taking Care of Yourself

Cleaning solvents like methyl ethyl ketone, carbon tetrachloride, toluene, trichloroethylene and benzene are carcinogenic. Even white spirit is a hazardous substance – in contact with the skin it is absorbed quickly into the bloodstream. The use of gloves is obvious, though, if not feasible, barrier cream on the hands may avert any adverse reaction that can occur with some solvents and also epoxy resin.

Consider calling in professional help for cleaning sails, or donning the full range of safety equipment, or leaving stains where they are. The use of goggles and a face mask or even breathing apparatus is not ridiculous.

Perhaps the best way of taking care of yourself is to spend your time out sailing rather than taking too much care of your sails, spars and rigging.

Summary

- Sails last longer if they are not allowed to flog in the wind. They retain their shape better if flaked or rolled. At intervals, sails should be washed and stains can be removed using appropriate solvents.

- Sail repairs should involve minimal disturbance to the body of the sail. Patches should be kept to minimum size, and wholesale replacement of panels is not recommended.

- The mast, rigging and fittings need to be cleaned and checked at intervals for fatigue, damage, poor operation and corrosion, repairing and replacing as necessary in some cases even if apparently sound.

- Fittings not functioning properly can often be repaired following dismantling. Familiarization with the operation of components aids problem-solving skills.

- Ignore the stains and go sailing!

GLOSSARY

Cross-references to other glossary entries are set in italic type.

Aft-swept rig A *rig* in which the *spreaders* are angled aft and the *cap* and *lower shroud chainplates* are placed aft of the mast position.

Alloy The combination of a metal with other metals and elements.

Angle of attack The angle between the direction of flow (of air or water) towards a *foil* and a straight line from the leading edge to the trailing edge of the foil.

Anodizing The production of an artificial oxide layer on the surface of aluminium *alloy* in order to improve corrosion resistance.

Apparent wind The wind speed and direction felt on board, which changes with the boat's speed and course and the *true wind* speed.

Aramid fibre A generic term for a particularly strong polymer fibre.

Aspect ratio The ratio of height and average width of a sail or other *foil.*

Asymmetric spinnaker A *spinnaker* that has a single luff and is built so that it will function as a very full *foresail* although it is not attached to the *forestay.*

Baby Stay See *inner forestay*

Backstay A *stay* that supports a mast from aft.

Backwind The effect in which one sail ahead of another bends the wind into the aft sail, thus changing its *angle of attack* and preventing the aft sail from setting properly.

Balance (when sailing) The ability of a boat to stay on course, usually when sailing *upwind*, without having to apply undesirable *helm.*

Barber hauler A system enabling the run of a *sheet* to be pulled outboard, increasing the effective *sheeting angle.*

Batten A strip of stiff material (commonly wood or reinforced resin) used to support the aft part of a sail. May extend from *leech* to *luff.*

Bermudan rig A *rig* having a *mainsail* that is essentially triangular in *planform.*

Bias A direction in which a cloth stretches more readily. The term often refers to an angle of 45° to the *warp* and *weft.*

Block A fitting into which a *sheave* is installed in order to provide the means for changing the *lead* of a rope.

Bolt rope A fibre rope or cord attached to the *luff* of a sail that allows the sail to be attached to a *spar* with a luff groove or to a *luff groove foil.*

Bottlescrew A screw device interposed between the *rigging* wire and *chainplates* in order to adjust the length of *shrouds* and *stays.*

Bowsprit A *spar* that overhangs the bow. When utilized on racing dinghies it is usually retractable.

Broaching Rounding into the wind uncontrollably under the influence of the wind and/or the waves.

Broad-seaming The sail-making process

in which seams are shaped in order to induce *camber* in a sail.

Buckle The failure of a *strut* by bending.

Burst bag A long, zippered bag for containing a *foresail.* The zipper is designed to pull apart readily.

Calendering Passing cloth between rollers under high pressure.

Camber Curvature in the horizontal plane of a sail. The term may be applied to *foils* generally.

Camber inducers Plastic extensions to *full-length battens* that enable them readily to flop from one side of the sail to the other, achieving the effect of a *rotating asymmetrical aerofoil.*

Cap shrouds As *main shrouds.*

Cascade system A system in which a *tackle,* usually two-*part,* is used to haul another tackle.

Centreboard An unballasted *keel foil* that can be lowered and raised about a pivot point.

Centre of buoyancy The position at which the force of buoyancy acts. (More correctly, the *centre of gravity* of the water displaced by the boat.)

Centre of gravity The position at which all weight could be considered to act.

Chafe patches Patches of sailcloth applied to a sail in areas likely to chafe against stanchions, *spreaders* and so on.

Chainplate A fitting on the deck edge or deck to which a *shroud* or *stay* is attached.

Check stays *Backstays* that support the middle part of the mast.

Chord length The distance from leading edge to trailing edge of a *foil* (*luff* to *leech* of a sail) at a horizontal position, which is relevant to the measurement of *camber.*

Clevis pin A pin that passes through a pair of plates and to which *rigging* is attached.

Clew The lower aft corner of a sail.

Column, out of The description of a *strut* that is bent, the bend being encouraged by the end loads.

Compression The result of end loads that act towards the middle of a column.

Crimp The undulation of *yarns* in a cloth caused by the weaving together of the *warp* and *weft.*

Cross-cut The *cut* of a sail in which the cloth *panel* seams essentially are perpendicular to the *leech.*

Cruising 'chute A sail that is fuller than a *foresail* and flatter than a *spinnaker,* and is *tacked* at the bow.

Cunningham hole An *eye* located a short distance above the *tack* of a sail so that the *luff* can be tensioned, usually when the sail can be hoisted no further.

Cupping The curling of the *leech* of a sail, usually a *foresail.*

Cut (of a sail) The arrangement of the *panels* of cloth and the means for providing *camber* in a sail.

Cutter A sailing yacht with two sails set on *stays* in front of the mast.

Density Mass per unit volume of a material.

De-powering (the rig) A means for reducing the force, in particular the side force, produced by the sails.

Diamond shrouds The two *shrouds,* self-contained on the mast, running over a *strut* and forming a diamond shape.

Diamond struts *Struts* over which *diamond shrouds* run.

Discontinuous rigging *Rigging* that is joined by links at the *spreader* ends.

Double-spreader rig A *rig* using two sets of *spreaders.*

Downwind, sailing Sailing with the wind behind the boat (though not necessarily directly behind).

Draft The maximum depth of the *camber* of a sail at a particular height.

Drum and axle A system for providing mechanical advantage in which wire rope is wound around an axle and tightened by a line on an interconnected drum.

Dyform *Standing rigging* wire in which the stainless steel strands are shaped so that they pack closely together.

Exotic materials The term used to describe materials having especially high strength- or stiffness-to-weight or stiffness characteristics.

Extrusion A long length of a required section (which may be hollow) formed by a process in which a semi-molten billet of metal is pushed through a shaped die or former.

Eye A reinforced hole formed in a sail, or a loop in fibre or wire rope.

Ferrule A sleeve that is compressed onto wire rope turned back on itself to form an *eye*.

Fine tune A system in which one end of the *mainsheet* attaches to a further *tackle*, like a *cascade system*, in order to provide a means of fine adjustment.

Flaking (sails) Folding a sail in concertina fashion.

Flattening reef An *eye* formed above the *clew* of the *mainsail*. In strong winds the eye is pulled downwards and aft.

Foil 1. A system, such as a sail or keel, that produces an element of force perpendicular to the direction of the wind or water. 2. A streamlined fairing such as is used for a *luff groove foil*.

Foot The bottom edge of a sail.

Foresail The fore-and-aft sail set forward of the mast and attached to the *forestay* (usually).

Forestay Forwardmost *stay* to which the

foresail is hanked or attached.

Fractional rig A *rig* in which the *forestay* meets the mast at a position below the top of the mast.

Full-length batten A *batten* that runs from the *leech* to the *luff* of a sail.

Fully battened sail A sail in which all *battens* are full-length.

Gaff A *spar* that projects the upper edge of a *gaff* sail and attaches at its inner end to the upper part of the mast.

Gaff rig A *rig* having a *mainsail* that is four-sided in profile.

Galvanic corrosion Corrosion that occurs when two different metals produce a small current flow between them in the presence of moisture or sea water.

Genoa A *foresail* (usually the largest) that overlaps the mast substantially.

Gunter rig A *rig* that uses a *gaff* hoisted close and parallel to the mast, resulting in a sail that is virtually triangular in profile.

Guy A rope that holds the *tack* of the *spinnaker* and the *spinnaker pole* in place.

Gybing Changing from one tack to another by turning the stern through the wind.

Halyard A fibre or wire rope used to hoist sails.

Hanks Fittings spaced along the *luff* of the *foresail* in order to attach the sail to the *forestay*.

Head 1. The top corner of a triangular sail. 2. The edge of a *gaff* sail that attaches to the gaff.

Heat-setting Passing cloth through ovens at high temperature.

Heat treatment A process in which the strength of a metal *alloy* can be enhanced.

Heel The bottom of a mast.

Helm The angle of rudder applied in

order that a boat will either maintain its course or turn.

Horizontal-cut A *spinnaker* cut with horizontal *panels*, little used today.

Hot-knife A tool for cutting and sealing the edges of polyester and nylon sailcloth.

Inner forestay (baby stay) An additional, shorter *forestay* attached to the mast and foredeck.

Intermediate shroud A *shroud* running from the deck to the lower *spreader* of a *double spreader rig* and then to the mast.

Jib The forward sail of a *cutter*.

Jumper stays The *stays* that provide control of the top part of the mast.

Jumper struts The *struts* that displace the *jumper stays.*

Keel foil The lateral area projecting below the hull of a yacht, other than the rudder, that resists *leeway.*

Ketch A two-masted *rig* in which the *mizzenmast* is stepped forward of the rudder (strictly speaking, the rudder pivot).

Kicking strap A system for preventing the boom rising when wind is in the sail.

Knit A fabric in which two layers of *yarns* are laid at 90 degrees to each other and held together with a cross-woven thread.

Lead The direction in which a rope runs.

Leech The trailing or aft edge of a sail.

Leech line A cord led through the leech *tabling* from head to clew.

Lee helm The tendency of a boat to turn away from the wind, corrected by holding the tiller *to leeward.*

Leeward, to Away from the wind.

Leeway The sideways drift of a boat caused by the wind in the sails, most noticeable when sailing *upwind.*

Loose-footed A boomed sail, usually a *mainsail*, attached at the *tack* and *clew* but not along the *foot.*

Lower shrouds The *shrouds* that support the lower part of the mast and in particular restrain the thrust produced by the lower *spreaders.*

Luff The leading edge of a sail.

Luffing Changing the boat's heading towards the wind.

Luff groove foil A system of low windage for attaching the *foresail* along its entire length to the *forestay.*

Mainsail The principal sail attached at its *luff* to the tallest mast.

Mainsheet The *sheet* for the *mainsail.*

Mainsheet hoop A structure, taking a hoop form, that raises the position of the *mainsheet block* from which the *mainsail* is sheeted.

Mainsheet track A track carrying a *mainsheet traveller,* permitting athwartships adjustment of the *mainsheet block.*

Mainsheet traveller A sliding attachment point on a *mainsheet track.*

Main shrouds The *shrouds* that intersect the mast at or in the vicinity of the position of the *forestay* intersection.

Masthead rig A *rig* in which the *foresail* is hoisted to the top of the mast.

Mast inversion The bending aft of the middle of the mast.

Mast track A track extending from the boom to the top of the mast in which *sail slides* run.

Mitre-cut The *cut* of a sail in which the *panels* are arranged so that they are perpendicular to both *leech* and *foot*, producing a seam from the *clew* to the *luff.*

Mizzen The sail set on the *mizzenmast.*

Mizzenmast The shorter, after mast of a *ketch* or *yawl*.

Mizzen staysail A sail hoisted from and *tacked* forward of the *mizzenmast*.

Modulus A measure of the response of a material to loading.

Multiple-spreader rig A *rig* using two or more sets of *spreaders*.

Muscle box A term used to describe a *tackle* comprising many *parts*.

Nobility A relative measure of the tendency of a metal to suffer *galvanic corrosion*.

Over-rotating mast A mast that is able to rotate to a selected angle to the boom.

Panel 1. The term used to describe a length of a *stayed* mast between *rigging* or *spreader* attachments or the deck support, liable to *buckling* 2. An element of a sail, often the width of the cloth on the roll, joined by seams.

Part (of a tackle) A line running from a *sheave* on one *block* to a sheave on the other block, forming a *tackle*.

Patches The pieces of cloth used in the corners of sails in order to provide additional reinforcement.

Peak The top corner of a *gaff* sail.

Pelican hook A hinged hook that can be opened fairly readily and detached from a *chainplate* or other fixing point.

Pitch The tendency of a yacht to hobby-horse when sailing into oncoming seas.

Planform The profile of a *foil* (or sail).

Pre-feeder A separate, lower section of *mast track* enabling a *mainsail* (usually) to be fed onto the track from *tack* to *head*, whereupon the sail can be hoisted.

Radial-cut The *cut* of a sail in which the *panels* radiate in order to deal with the tensions in the cloth.

Radial-head cut A *spinnaker* with the upper third cut *radially* and the lower two-thirds cut *horizontally*.

Rake (of mast) The lean of the mast, usually aft, measured either as an angle or in terms of the distance the top of the mast lies aft of the mast at deck or coachroof level.

Ratchet block A block in which the *sheave* is ratcheted to permit one way rotation only.

Rig 1. A way of describing a sailing boat according to the *planform* of the sails. 2. All the sails, *spars* and *rigging*.

Rigging All the ropes used to support the mast and control the sails.

Roach The round of the aft edge of a sail that extends beyond a straight line from the *clew* to the *head*.

Roll The periodic rotational movement of a boat from side to side.

Rope stopper A device that serves as a means of restraining a fibre rope but can be released readily.

Rotating asymmetrical foil (RAF) A rather grandiose term used to describe a *fully battened* sail in which the *battens* flop to *leeward* improving airflow on the leeward side of the sail.

Running backstays *Backstays* that are adjustable when sailing.

Running rigging Ropes, either of fibre or wire, that are adjustable and used to set or control the sails and mast.

Sacrificial strip (sail) A strip of cloth with a high resistance to ultra-violet light, sewn to both the *leech* and *foot* of a *foresail* designed to be furled, in order to protect the sail.

Sail-maker's palm A leather strap worn on the hand, containing an indented metal plate used to push a needle through thick sailcloth.

Sail plan The drawing of the profile of the sails as if pulled into the centre-line of the boat.

Sail slides Attachments sewn or fastened to a sail, usually the *mainsail*, that slide in the *mast track.*

Schooner rig A *rig* having two (or more) masts, the aft one being of the same height or taller than the forward mast.

Scouring The process for cleaning woven cloth in a detergent bath to remove the *sizes.*

Scotch-cut The *cut* of a sail in which the seams of the cloth *panels* are parallel to the *leech.*

Scrims Open weave cloths with visible spaces between the *yarns.*

Section The outline of a cutting plane. For a mast, the shape formed by the walls of the mast when sliced horizontally.

Self-tailing winch A winch that can be used without hauling the *sheet* by hand.

Selvedge The woven edge of a cloth.

Semi-radial cut The cut of a radial sail in which some cloth *panels* are arranged at a constant angle to the *luff* for more consistent luff stretch characteristics.

Sheave A grooved wheel contained within a *block* or in a *spar* that changes the *lead* of a fibre or wire rope.

Sheeting (sails) Pulling in the sails.

Sheeting angle The angle between the boat's centre-line and a straight line from the *tack* of the *foresail* to its *sheeting* position.

Sheets Ropes used to pull the sails towards the centre-line or to free them.

Shroud angle The angle between a *shroud*, usually a *cap shroud*, and the mast.

Shroud base The horizontal distance from the mast to the *shroud chainplate* on one side of the boat.

Shrouds *Rigging* that supports the mast athwartships.

Sizes Lubricants to assist the cloth-weaving process.

Sleeved luff The *luff* of a sail in which a sleeve is formed to slide over the mast.

Sloop A sailing yacht or dinghy with a *mainsail* and a *foresail.*

Snubbing winch A rotating drum on which a *sheet* may be wound. The drum is ratcheted to permit clockwise rotation only but no mechanical advantage is given.

Soft sail A sail in which the *battens* are not full-length, except perhaps the top batten.

Span An element of a *shroud* which spans points of attachment at the mast, deck or *spreaders.*

Spars Poles that support the sails.

Spinnaker A sail that has more *camber* than a *foresail*, set forward of the *forestay* and used when the wind is from astern and from abeam.

Spinnaker pole A *spar* used to project the *tack* of a *spinnaker.*

Spreaders *Struts* that spread the *shrouds*, thus improving the *shroud angle.*

Standing rigging *Rigging* that supports the mast and is not adjusted whilst sailing.

Star-cut spinnaker A flat, radially cut *spinnaker* designed for sailing with the wind abeam.

Stays *Rigging* that supports the mast fore and aft.

Staysail A sail set immediately in front of the mast on a *cutter.*

Stiff 1. The term applied to a yacht that does not heel readily. 2. The tendency of a material not to deflect readily when loaded.

Stress The amount of loading occurring at a position within a material relative to the amount of material resisting the loading.

Stress concentration A position in a structure at which *stress* is increased because a discontinuity, such as an internal corner, exists.

Strops (mainsheet) A system in which lengths of rope from each side of a dinghy are used to adjust the position of the *mainsheet block.*

Structured cloth Resin film-based sailcloth that is highly stable.

Strut A column in *compression* that *buckles* when the load is sufficiently high.

Swaged terminal An *eye* formed in the end of a wire rope using *swages* and a *ferrule.*

Swages Shaped metal *blocks* used to squeeze a *ferrule* onto wire rope.

Tabling The folded edge or applied tape on the edge of a sail to provide reinforcement and, in the case of the *leech*, to contain the *leech-line.*

Tack 1. The lower forward corner of a sail 2. To attach the tack of a sail to the deck or coachroof. 3. A sailing boat is on a tack when not in the process of *gybing* or *tacking.*

Tacking Changing from one *tack* to the other by turning the bow through the wind.

Tacking downwind The technique whereby a *downwind* objective can be reached most quickly by *gybing* onto alternate *tacks* and sailing at an angle to the wind.

Tackle A system of *blocks* and line.

Tang A plate fastened to a mast to which *rigging* is attached.

Tell-tales Strips of lightweight cloth or wool attached to sails to indicate the nature of the air flow over the sails.

Tender The tendency of a yacht to heel readily.

Tension mapping Representation of the tensions occurring in a sail (in particular).

Terminal A fitting at the end of a *shroud* or *stay* by which it can be attached to the mast, a *tang* or a *bottlescrew.*

Thimble A metal *eye* reinforcement for wire or fibre rope.

Throat The corner of a *gaff* sail between the *head* and the *luff.*

Tri-radial cut A *spinnaker* for which the *panel* layout radiates from each corner but with horizontal panels in the middle of the sail.

True wind Wind speed and direction measured when not moving.

Twist The falling away to *leeward* of a sail towards its *head.*

Una rig A *rig* with a *mainsail* only.

Upwind, sailing Sailing as close to the wind as possible such that best progress towards the wind is made.

Velocity ratio The ratio of the length of line hauled and the distance moved by the loaded part of a *tackle.*

Vortex A swirl of air (or water) occurring at the tip of an aerofoil (or hydrofoil).

Warp *Yarns* running along the length of the cloth.

Weather, to Towards the wind.

Weather helm The tendency of a boat to turn towards the wind, which is corrected by holding the tiller *to weather.*

Weft *Yarns* running across the width of the cloth, when woven.

Windward, to Towards the wind.

Wings Lateral extensions at the bottom of a keel *foil.*

Yarn Fibres twisted together. A thread.

Yawl A two-masted rig for which the *mizzenmast* is stepped aft of the rudder (strictly speaking, the rudder pivot).

INDEX